Endorsements and Praise for *God Our Anchor*

God Our Anchor is a riveting read that takes on one of the most volatile attacks on the family and the church. No family is safe from the attack of drug addiction, and Deborah Bailey takes this issue head-on pulling no punches. This biblically sound devotional is a must-read not only for those who are in the battle but also to prepare for the possibility of an upcoming battle. *God Our Anchor* sheds light on who is behind the attack and why we must be anchored to the hope found only in Christ.

Rick Burgess
cohost of *The Rick and Bubba Show*

For parents facing the gut-wrenching but all-too-common experience of walking through their children's drug addictions, Deborah Bailey's *God Our Anchor* provides the tools to wholly align their thinking on this difficult life experience with God's perspective. Seeing it God's way is practically the whole battle, and *God Our Anchor* gets you there.

Mark Pettus
Highlands College

Addiction never only affects the user; it always touches the family members of the addict. *God Our Anchor* reminds us not to place our hope in the answers offered to us by the world but rather to tether our souls to trusting in our loving God. Deborah has provided a great source of comfort, peace, and direction for heartbroken and distraught parents looking for answers and hope.

Micah Andrews
chief executive officer, The Foundry Ministries
Bessemer, Alabama

As a pastor, counselor, and Christian addiction specialist, I highly recommend *God Our Anchor* as a must-read for every Christian parent who is struggling with a prodigal child mired in drugs, alcohol, and other rebellious activities. Deborah has touched on every aspect of pain and healing a parent goes through, whether married or single, while dealing with addictions in their family. This book is a great tool as study guide for support groups across America.

Rock Hobbs
senior pastor/executive director, Transformation Ministries
Birmingham, Alabama

GOD
OUR
ANCHOR

A 30-DAY DEVOTIONAL

GOD OUR ANCHOR

HELD FAST THROUGH A
LOVED ONE'S ADDICTION

Deborah Bailey

PUBLISHING GROUP

NASHVILLE, TENNESSEE

Dedication

I dedicate this book first to my Father, my Savior and my constant Companion. Lord, You inspired me to write this book, and I am grateful for the healing it has brought me.

I dedicate this book second to families in the storm of addiction. May God be ever present and your anchor along your journey as well.

Lastly, I dedicate this book to my husband and my son, who both encouraged me, believed in me, and stood by me when continuing was tough. The struggle present during the writing only proved that it needed to be completed and shared.

Contents

Introduction 1
Ashlynn's Story 5

Part I: Batten Down the Hatches 13

Day 1: Marriage Shaking 15
Day 2: Boundaries 21
Day 3: Lack of Trust 27
Day 4: Advice from Others 32
Day 5: Giving Your Child to God 36
Day 6: Constant Prayer 41
Day 7: Love 45

Part II: Throwing in the Anchor 51

Day 8: Anger 53
Day 9: Guilt 58
Day 10: Forgiveness 62
Day 11: Fear 68
Day 12: Strength 72
Day 13: Spiritual Warfare 77

Day 14: Worry and Anxiety 82
Day 15: Sleeplessness 87
Day 16: Pain and Suffering 91
Day 17: Apathetic and Empty 97
Day 18: Where Are You, God? 101
Day 19: Lack of Faith...........................107
Day 20: Hopelessness...........................110
Day 21: Listening..............................114
Day 22: Disappointment.........................119
Day 23: Speak Life.............................123

Part III: Anchored.................................129

Day 24: Who Is My God? 131
Day 25: Joy 135
Day 26: Thankfulness 139
Day 27: Understanding..........................144
Day 28: Running the Race.......................148
Day 29: God's Plan.............................152
Day 30: God's Knowledge 155

Afterword 159
About the Author 163

Introduction

*Fearing we might run aground on the rocks, they dropped
four anchors from the stern and prayed for daylight to come.*

ACTS 27:29

In Acts chapter 27, Paul and some other men encountered massive storms at sea which battered their ship. One night Paul heard from an angel of God who said, "Do not give up." Paul knew they would probably shipwreck somewhere, but he also believed God would see them through to the end. Paul and these men did all they could do physically by throwing over four anchors, and then they did what they could do spiritually; they prayed, knowing their primary anchor was God.

Anchors signify a major point in our lives, as we battled the storm of a child addict. But to completely understand this point, you need to know the definition of the word *anchor*:

An anchor is a heavy object attached to a rope or chain and used to moor a vessel to the sea bottom. It can also be a person or thing that provides stability or confidence in an otherwise uncertain situation.
(Oxford Dictionary)

As sailors encounter storms at sea, so we encounter storms in our lives. Some will be worse than others. When the storms first rocked our boat, I was a forty-three-year-old, happily married, Christian mother of two beautiful children: a girl of sixteen and a twelve-year-old boy. I was in an enjoyable, fulfilling, and flexible job in the medical profession. It sounds like I had a perfect life and had my act together, doesn't it? But nothing was further from the truth. It was the calm before the storm. I made a beautiful picture because being a Christian means everything in life is perfect, right? At least that is how most of us pretend to act around others, especially when we are with our church family.

As a person of faith, I had a hard time admitting to the church, family, and friends about nasty, personal storms. I had to choose honesty rather than running from the truth and life God had blessed me with so graciously. Christians are never promised a perfect life here on earth. That is what we will find in heaven! In fact, that is how heaven is now. However, we are still on earth with severe, sorrow-proclaiming storms and trials. I have had many little life storms, but this storm, starting when life looked perfect, was one of the biggest trials of my existence.

My daughter, who loved God and led others to God, was becoming a prodigal child. She was wasting away the gifts the

Lord had given her. At sixteen she was making choices that affected not only her but everyone in her life. Her rebellion started off as regular teenage disrespect and disobedience, but she crossed the line, and the storm blew out of control in our family. Soon drugs, alcohol, and complete fits of rage entered our home. Drug addiction is a terrible storm that rips apart everyone in its path. It is a monstrosity! It rocks and batters your child and the entire family. As a parent, you may often feel like you will sink and drown in the storm, but, rest assured, you are safe when you keep your eyes on the Master.

While I could write a fascinating book on our family life over the last few years, that is not what God has led me to do. Through my experiences I have found no profound solutions for how parents can rescue their child from drug addiction. I have read many books, attended counseling, and met with various medical professionals for my child. Family and friends have given advice, and I have learned a lot from the godly counsel I received, but that is not what helped me most in this storm. The one who rescued me is God. I found my peace through anchoring myself in His Word, through prayer time with my precious Healer, Protector, and Savior, and through constant worship.

God "whispered" to me a little over three years ago that I should write a book about my experience to share with others going through a similar storm. In fact, God led me to write a book of devotions to help other parents have Scripture in their hands to help them through parenting a wayward, drug-addicted child. Prayer and knowledge of God's Word are powerful battle tools. Both tools elevate authority over our troubles and raise our trust and faith in God. I let God lead me, desiring to be only a vessel for His Word. Readers can feel the emotions from my experiences during these times. Feelings and emotions can get the best of our soul and body until we are as strung out as our addict child. But through prayer and Scripture, a parent can stand firm and grow in faith through the storm of addiction.

My desire through these devotions is that you find peace, joy, and once again sense God's love and grace through your storm of parenting a drug-addicted child. My prayer is that you will become anchored by God's presence, His promises, and His Word. I pray that you will no longer allow the raging storm of drug addiction to toss you to and fro to the point where you cannot see God or feel His presence. And, if you do not know Jesus as your Savior, I pray you will submit everything to Him and allow Jesus to carry you through this storm. Finally, I pray that if you are already a Christian you will renew your trust in God and not permit this storm to become bigger than your God.

As you begin this journey with me, I would like to share Ashlynn's story. Her story is important because it shines a light on the source of all battles with addiction. The fight is against sin, not your child. Satan is our enemy and the one who seeks to steal and destroy anyone in any way to prevent God's glory and power from being revealed in this world. He uses drugs and addiction as weapons of attack. As you read Ashlynn's story, you can see how even before we realized it, the devil had already been scheming in our lives to wreak havoc and pull us away from God.

Ashlynn's Story

Beautiful, blue-eyed Ashlynn Nicole Bailey was born April 21, 1995, to proud parents Mike and Deborah Bailey. She had to stay in the step-down unit after birth because she required medical treatment for pneumonia after aspiration during the delivery process. Ashlynn was tiny but a fighter and stayed strong during the healing process. She had to stay in the hospital for seven days before we could bring her home. We all instantly fell in love with her, our first child and the first grandchild on both sides of our family. We had to be careful about allowing Ashlynn to be around people soon after her birth due to her having pneumonia; but as soon as she could attend church, we had her there. She was dedicated at about eight months in our church's parent-baby dedication ceremony. Growing up in church, Ashlynn learned about God and became a Christian at an early age. She loved God, felt that everyone needed to go to heaven, and even led several of her friends to Christ.

Ashlynn loved people, adventures, having fun, and celebrating life. She was fun spirited and never wanted to miss out on anything. Ashlynn's main struggle as a toddler and young child was handling her anger. She was usually happy, but when she got upset, she was upset! She was nearly impossible to console once she reached this point and would have to just calm herself down in her room alone. I mention this because it is important later in her life story. Ashlynn loved school but had a few misfortunate events early in life that created a personal wound to her soul. She was a tiny little girl, much smaller than most children her age (but not much different from how her mom was as a baby and child). During her first few days of public kindergarten, she was ridiculed for being short. Girls would not let her in their club because she was "too small" to be in school. She came home heartbroken, and so were her mom and dad. We parented her through this the best way we knew how, but unfortunately she would continue to be labeled as "short," "tiny," and "little" even throughout high school.

From the age of about seven years old, Ashlynn wanted to be a cheerleader. She took dance lessons and gymnastics to help prepare her and began working on her cheerleading skills when she was in the sixth grade. In seventh grade Ashlynn tried out for middle school cheerleading and made it! She cried tears of joy when she found out; she could not believe it. As parents we thought this would help bring her the confidence she needed to overcome the low self-esteem she developed over being so little. Ashlynn continued to cheer through her sophomore year in high school and was on a competitive cheer team as well during those middle school and high school years.

During this time she was still kidded about being little, but she learned different coping methods to handle what she was feeling inside. She built up a tough outer exterior, but on the inside I think it still crushed her. Ashlynn loved cheering, and you could not keep her away from practice! Once she was in high school, she decided she might even like to pursue cheering in college. An excellent, sweet coach she had on the competitive team encouraged her with her size because most college cheerleaders needed to be small to be "flyers."

During Ashlynn's freshman year in high school, we saw noticeable changes in her behavior. Many of her friends changed, her grades declined from all A's to A's, B's, and a C here or there, and her desire to cheer and attend practice decreased. As parents we suspected possible drug use, but we could never find evidence. We prayed for God to reveal the truth to us, and He did in two ways. First, I (her mom) awakened from a deep sleep one night to the sound of God's voice saying, "Your child is doing drugs." Second, a few days following that, she was drug tested at school and came home upset she would fail. Initially she told us that it was her first time trying "weed." Later we came to find out she had been experimenting previously as well. We believe she was trying marijuana to fit in with her friends. Ashlynn was trying to show others she was "big enough." We think the marijuana made her feel euphoric and like she was in control. We believe it made her feel like she had no pain and no anger. That would just be the beginning.

As much as we tried to stay on top of this situation as parents, things spiraled out of control. It was simply an awful, gut-wrenching experience! She quit cheerleading by the end of her sophomore year. By then her grades were plummeting, and she and her friends were constantly in trouble. Some of her good friends were pushing away from her, her anger and mood swings were beyond manageable, we received phone calls from the police, and she was arrested—just one thing after another. She never graduated from high school because she went to rehab the last two months of her senior year. She did well in this rehab program, came home, and took the GED before attending college for a brief time. The demon of drug addiction struck again.

Through counseling sessions at the first rehab, we learned that Ashlynn had a terrible misfortune happen to her during high school, and she never got over it. She used drugs to hide her pain and her self-hate. While she had tried most every kind of drug, heroin was the hook, line, and sinker—her drug of choice. It is a tough drug to rehab from, especially in a real addict's brain. Looking back at Ashlynn's life and personality, we believe she had addictive tendencies all along, and it took one time of the right drug for her to be hooked on it forever, with the constant craving of that first experience with heroin. We believe the devil used the drugs to devour Ashlynn because he knew she could be a great Christian warrior. She was a threat to him, and he went after her with a vengeance. As a family, we claimed the verse Jeremiah 29:11 over her life and our life: "'For I know the plans that I have for you,' declares the LORD, 'plans for welfare and not for calamity to give you a future and a hope'" (NASB). We were going to hold onto God's Word no matter what the devil was throwing at us.

Over the course of several more years, Ashlynn was in and out of various rehabs. She would have brief moments of victory over her addiction. She even tried to start school again at a junior college. Ashlynn so wanted a better life for herself. She wanted to pursue a career that would help others, but addiction would eventually win. She thought she had ruined her life forever and could not seem to figure out how to start over. Ashlynn did not want to be an addict and would often state she wished she had never tried drugs. She prayed and prayed for the addiction to be taken away. She wanted to be healed instantly from the addiction! Ashlynn was under much prayer during these tumultuous years. God was reaching out to Ashlynn in many ways, but she could not see it because she believed the devil's lies. Ashlynn eventually fell into a dark place—we think she felt that her life was hopeless and that she would never be healed of the disease; we believe she felt God had given up on her, which was what the devil wanted her to believe. It's hard to see your child in this degree of despair without being pulled into the pit yourself.

A Parent's Journey

As a parent, each of us has hopes and dreams for our child. We want the best for them and for them to seek the best out of life. We work hard to provide, teach, mentor, and love our child. Parenting is an incredible, exhausting full-time job. When something like drug addiction comes along, it crushes dreams, creates doubt in our parenting skills, causes us to develop feelings toward our child and those close to us we have never had before, and it can even cause us to question our faith. It causes us to question our God. Can you see how the devil is using drug addiction not only to destroy your child but to destroy you as well?

Having a child that is a drug addict will produce some crazy out-of-control emotions, thoughts, and conflicts that affect not only you personally but others as well. These emotions, thoughts, and conflicts will create an inner personal turmoil and sleeplessness.

The truth is, you won't even know who you are anymore if you let these issues rule your life. Your relationship with your child and spouse will suffer. Your relationships with your other children, your parents, and even your friends can be negatively affected. You will feel misunderstood, desperate, and you will pine for your old life before your child used drugs. And, while you will be willing to do most anything to stop your child from doing drugs, you can even become an enabler, which isn't what your child needs. Before long you will isolate yourself from others, and you may even separate yourself from God. Depression sets in and apathy rules because you cannot see how things could possibly get any better. You may find yourself in a deep, dark pit and not know how to get out. If so, you have fallen for Satan's scheme, you have listened to his lies, and you believe them. Satan has you right where he wants you.

You cannot help your child, you cannot help yourself, and life has become a mess. All you need is someone to understand, someone to change everything, someone to make things right again, someone to give you peace, strength, and redemption from the pain and sorrow. Jesus is the only person who can do all of this, and somehow you must cry out to Him. You must lay down everything, including your child, at the foot of the cross—a complete surrender of all. Then you must seek Him, praise Him, and worship Him—repenting for allowing the storm of drug addiction to become bigger than God. Turn your focus on Jesus alone. Jesus never left you. You were pulled astray by the devil's schemes and lies, and you have been trying to fix everything on your own. You must reach the end of yourself before being willing to reach out for help—just as the person addicted to drugs. Only then can Christ resurrect us from our lowest and messiest of places.

As you read through these devotions, Scriptures, and prayers, seek God with all your heart. Ask Him for His help, and you will find it. You will see your faith grow and watch God deliver you from the dark pit. You will become the parent your child battling addiction needs. God's work in this storm will be obvious to your child and everyone around you. You will be anchored in the midst of your storm.

PART I

Batten Down the Hatches

In a storm, sailors will prepare the ship for the surge to come, often referred to as "battening down the hatches." As you look out and see the storm on the horizon, you must "batten down" critical areas. Follow me on a journey of preparation for this storm of addiction.

Marriage Shaking

> *"For this reason a man will leave his father and mother
> and be united to his wife, and the two will become one
> flesh. So they are no longer two, but one flesh. Therefore
> what God has joined together, let no one separate."*
>
> MARK 10:7–9 NIV

I am no expert in parenting nor an expert in marriage. The words I write are a result of spending time in prayer and studying God's Word and based on the experiences I have gone through in my marriage dealing with a rebellious teen battling a drug addiction. I preface what I say with this: marriage is complicated enough without other stresses added such as illness, disease, family, children, and careers. While all marriages should rely on God first, sometimes outside counseling is needed, and my intentions are not to provide this book as a substitute for professional counseling, nor is my role that of a counselor. The purpose of including marriage as a topic in this book is to share the experiences I have had and to demonstrate how keeping your marriage a priority is crucial in parenting a child addicted to drugs.

Each one of us is unique in personality, beliefs, and life experiences. When a person gets married, he or she brings that uniqueness into the marriage and is expected to merge with someone with differing personality traits. Our personalities, beliefs, and life experiences affect our thoughts and actions in parenting. These differences can be a source of conflict in marriage. But woe to the marriage impacted by a rebellious teen, let alone a drug addict in the midst! You better have God front and center, and the two of you better be acting and thinking like one!

My daughter developed many rebellious habits outside of drug abuse. In attempts to cover up her addiction, she became an expert at the manipulation game, and her best strategy was using one parent against the other. She would use the expression, "You always take dad's side" or "You love my brother more than me." When she was told no by one parent, she would go to the other parent and try to get the answer she wanted. This caused several marriage battles. Resentment was being built on all sides.

Thankfully, God does not intend our marriages to be run by our children. He intends for our marriages to founded by Him and through Him. He expects our marriages to be based on His Word. The husband is the head of the household and the spiritual leader of the family. The wife is the husband's "helper" and devoted to seeking the best for her family. With

God as the center of marriage, husband and wife become one entity. They should support each other, have each other's back, and love each other deeply. Children can never be placed above the sanctity of marriage. Marriage was a vow the two of you took before God. Children are a blessing from God for your marriage. When one of your children seeks to be rebellious, you must first go to God in prayer individually and then as a married couple. Decisions should only be made with God's input and based on His Word. At times you may differ in your approach. My suggestion is to let your husband be the household and spiritual leader. You, as his wife, come alongside and support his decisions and help him carry them out. Your children should know that they are loved, but certain boundaries must not be crossed within your marriage, and the two of you should work as one unit.

Make sure you and your husband spend time alone together to reconnect the love that is often stressed when raising children. Husbands court your wife, and wives flirt with your husband. Make each other feel special and needed. Have fun with each other. Do not rely on your spouse to be your source of joy, for only God can be that. During stressful times your spouse may seem distant or not there for you because of dealing with sadness and disappointment in raising a rebellious child. Make sure you are communicating these problems with your spouse. Misunderstanding something that is said or not said can build a high wall of resentment.

A child may often have negative traits similar to your spouse—little aggravating, pesky habits or attitudes you never noticed when the two of you were dating but pop up over time. You may not have even noticed them until they start coming out of your rebellious child. Then the child becomes "your child" instead of our child. Do not blame your spouse for behavioral problems your child is having! That only lessens your confidence in your spouse as a parent and destroys unity in the marriage. You are one, so insulting your spouse is also insulting yourself. Remember that neither your spouse nor your child is the enemy here. Seek God to correct your issues first and to provide wisdom and strength in raising your child. Be as one under God's direction. Your child, even though rebellious, will know that home and family are secure. Show them how God works in relationships and that the marriage vow is of Him, from Him, and for Him.

For individuals that are divorced or separated, still stand firm and united as parents of your child. Make every effort to put aside your differences. Seek God and respect each other out of the love and peace Christ grants to each one of us. Even though you may not be living as husband and wife, you are still parenting a child who needs the two of you to be united in the willingness to provide a source of stability. Work to find common ground on boundaries, disciplinary actions, and problem-solving efforts.

As for single parents, where there is not a second parent involved personally with the child, I strongly suggest having a trusted friend, mentor, or counselor you can confide in and seek godly advice. Parenting a child, especially one with drug addiction, should never be done alone. You will need support and counsel from others.

Dear Lord,

Thank You so much for my wonderful spouse! Thank You that my partner is such a wise and loving parent to our children. Thank You for the strength not to give up on our rebellious child and for the grace to love our child unconditionally, as You love us. Thank You that during trials and issues in opposing opinions You give us peace when we ask. Forgive us for not putting You first in our thoughts and decisions. Forgive us for any resentment we have built up, and replace it with respect and love. Thank You that even though our child may not have liked our team approach to our parenting the way we value our marriage will be evident. Keep our marriage safe from evil, rooted in unconditional love, and growing in You. Make us wise and loving parents to our child. Grant us peace during trials that may come. Strengthen our unity so our power in You increases.

Amen.

Questions for Thought

~ Are my spouse and I acting in one accord in the parenting of our addicted child?

~ Do my spouse and I communicate regularly (in a respectful, peaceful manner) the daily issues that arise with our wayward child? And with our discussion, are we problem solving to meet the needs of our child and not our own agendas?

~ Do my spouse and I pray together about our marriage? Our children? Do we seek God first in all we do as a married couple and as parents of a drug-addicted child?

~ Am I putting my child and this storm before my marriage? Am I neglecting the one I made a vow to be with "for better or for worse"? What efforts am I making to spend time reconnecting with my spouse as a married partner?

~ Am I, as a wife, trying to rule over my husband and take his place as the spiritual leader in our home? Am I nagging and complaining to him, or am I seeking ways to be his helper, gracefully and lovingly helping with the issues at hand? Am I, as a husband, trying to dictate my home under my own rules, or am I seeking God's will and wisdom in leading my home? Do I love my wife as Christ loves the church? Am I nurturing and protecting her?

Boundaries

You're blessed when you follow his directions, doing your best to find him. That's right—you don't go off on your own; you walk straight along the road he set. You, GOD, prescribed the right way to live; now you expect us to live it. Oh, that my steps might be steady, keeping to the course you set; then I'd never have any regrets in comparing my life with your counsel. I thank you for speaking straight from your heart; I learn the pattern of your righteous ways. I'm going to do what you tell me to do; don't ever walk off and leave me.

PSALM 119:2–8 MSG

I love these verses, especially the way The Message paraphrase of the Bible puts it. Directions for following boundaries are easily explained in this verse. This message from God, through David, is an excellent reminder for my children and each of us as parents. As a mother I want my children to obey me like this Scripture details. I can only imagine how easy life would be if my children walked the way I told them, followed my directions, and then thanked me for showing them the way. I would never have to discipline my children. That would be a wonderful life, but it rarely works out this way in parenting!

I believe we are blessed with freedom when we follow God's way and not our own way. When we walk the walk, no matter what our child does or how our child acts, we are demonstrating exactly what God expects. However, we often make the mistake of seeking our way instead of asking for God's direction. When we seek our own way in parenting, marriage, or anywhere in life, it separates us from the fullness God has for us. In my own situation I was the one that went off course. Once I realized the pit I had fallen in, I cried out to the Lord for help. God graciously rescued me and redirected my steps. My circumstances did not change, but I was choosing to be obedient to God's direction, and that makes a world of difference.

Family life runs smoother when each one of us is trying to walk in God's ways. When we stood by the principles of God's Word, we encountered opposition from our drug-addicted child. Now, it wasn't that my daughter was knowingly opposing God, but she was opposed to the rules we set as parents, the rules we adopted through God's Word. These are the same principles God gives us as His children—not to torment us and hold us prisoner but to guide us because He loves us and wants no harm to be bestowed upon us. As we grow closer to God, we want to obey His commands. Consequently, as we obey God, we are expressing love toward Him. My child, however, could not see that full obedience to God leads to blessings and freedom. Even though she was a child of God, she meandered off on her own path much like David and very much like Israel.

Drug addicts want their way because of an overwhelming bodily desire to satisfy the craving of their drug of choice. A drug addict's brain is truly not capable of making a rational decision. Right and wrong become clouded. They are in survival mode running on animal instinct to get what they need at all costs. Drug addicts are willing to go against their own family, authority, and God's ways to satisfy the drug craving.

As a parent of an addict, the relentless torture of watching the depravity of your child seeking drugs begins to wear on you mentally and emotionally. You are willing to do anything to make the craziness stop. I began to question if standing up for God's ways was helping my daughter. I even began to relax boundaries I thought I would never cross in my household just to have a little peace. But I did not get peace; instead more violent turmoil was a result. I decided to go off on my own to seek my own peace, and that is when things spiraled out of control. I had to get back on the path God designed me to follow if I was ever going to be able to help my daughter.

God does not change His laws to meet the needs of His people, especially when they get off course. Instead, He changes the people to become more like Him through a series of painful events. The painful events were not created by God. They are caused by the choices we make and the resulting consequences. God uses those results as a discipline tool. We must lean heavily on Him to get us through our consequences as we change direction and get back on the right path.

I came to a sobering realization: I could not change my daughter, and my husband could not either. As a couple—as parents—we resolved not to change our God-directed household rules. We set boundaries in place to protect our family and home. Here's what these boundaries do for our family:

These boundaries were formed out of love and to keep harm from each one in our family. These limits do not include the use of drugs within our household. Consequences and penalties are enacted when the guidelines are broken. Forgiveness, grace, and truth are ever present in the midst. A definitive boundary was drawn in the home; continued drug use without seeking any means of help would result in being removed from the family environment. As a minor our child had one choice—drug rehabilitation. As she became an adult, she had two options—one was drug rehabilitation, the other was living outside our home independently. These boundaries may sound cruel and inhumane, but it is a form of intervention to bring drug addicts to their senses.

In the Bible the parable of the prodigal child is similar. Just as the father in the parable of the prodigal child let his son leave, God will allow us out on our own, but He never leaves us. He is always right there waiting for our return home. We are free to choose to follow our own desires, but if we want to go against His ways, God will let us meander in the desert. He will implement any form of consequence to bring us back to Him because He loves us too much to leave us in our own misery. As a parent I am not abandoning my drug-addicted child. I have set before my child specific boundaries that have a consequence if crossed. My child is making a choice. I will never leave my child. I am always right here for my child to support and assist her when she is willing to be drug free. I am not here to allow her to continue to use drugs. I must rely on God's strength to keep these boundaries. As my child continues to go her own way, I place my faith in God that as my child seeks Him, He will transform her into the person He designed her to be. My prayer is she will choose His path and not continue in the wrong direction.

God is a God of order. Boundaries were given by God in the beginning in the garden of Eden because He knows our tendency to stray. We are only blessed with freedom, peace, joy, and fullness of life when we choose to walk in God's direction, stand up for God's laws, and live within God's loving boundaries. When we love God as He meant us to love Him, we will be obedient, and it will be easier to make the right choice.

> *Dear Lord,*
> *Thank You that You have a right path for us to follow, one that leads to freedom, peace, and closer to You. Thank You for not letting us stay lost in our way. Thank You for directing us back where we must go. Thank You for the challenging situations and pain we must endure to realize we are way off track. Thank You for the grace You give us. Thank You for being by*

our side—a compass for us to follow. Give us
strength and grace to stand for Your ways, Lord,
as we parent our wayward child. Grant us
wisdom as we develop boundaries of grace and
truth in our home. Give us the strength to protect
our boundaries when they are crossed. Give us
peace when we intervene with consequences for
boundaries crossed, knowing, Lord, that You
will never leave us or our child but that You are
always awaiting our return home.
Amen.

Questions for Thought

~ Have my spouse and I established boundaries
within our home that are in line with God's will
and God's guidelines?

~ Am I as a parent following God's boundaries, or
am I off on my own, meandering the desert?

~ Do each of my children, including my wayward
child, understand the importance of these boundaries? Do each of our children know that the
boundaries are established with truth and grace
and designed out of love to protect and nurture?
Do each of my children know the consequences of
crossing the boundaries?

Lack of Trust

> *It is better to take refuge in the LORD than to trust in humanity.*
> PSALM 118:8

Trust can be defined as "the reliance on the integrity, strength, and ability of a person or thing." Trust is developed with people based on the time we spend with them and in direct relationship to how those people respond to us when we need them to have integrity, when we need them to be strong for us, when we need an able body to be there. In modern terms trust is "having someone's back" and not compromising that relationship out of selfish ambition or needs.

As parents we never trust our newborns. We don't know what to expect from them. They trust us for everything even without knowing us for long. They cannot survive without what we can provide for them. Once our babies have reached a few months of age, they seem to know us as their family. They, in turn, act differently toward strangers. Some have called it "separation anxiety." I wonder, however, if maybe our babies trust us as parents because of the time we have spent with them to meet their needs, to be true, and to be dependable for them, whereas a stranger has not yet developed that trusting relationship with them.

As children grow, parents start to trust them as individuals. As parents, our trust grows out of our child's integrity. Will children act the way they should even when we are not there directly providing supervision? As our children make wise decisions and obey us as parents, we begin to entrust them with more responsibilities and activities. Once a child deviates from obedience and makes a poor decision, our trust of that child erodes. As parents we usually discipline the child's erroneous behavior or action, and with time we start to build that trust relationship again if the child continues to obey us and continues to show integrity when we are not present.

Trusting a wayward, rebellious child, a child in bondage to drugs is a challenge. Without trust any relationship will deteriorate. Even though children may behave wrongly, they still need us to trust them and believe in them. And we need to be able to trust our child. The lack of trusting my child created an anxiety, a fear of the unknown, and a sense of failure in my parenting skills. These feelings are from the devil to steal my joy and hope that Christ has promised me and has given to me.

All parents go through the trust-building process with any child, but I must address the uniqueness of the situation with a wayward child, especially with an addict. Wayward children want their own way no matter what. Their own needs and desires are more important than anything else. You may have experienced a child who will say and do anything to survive and to fulfill a drug need. Addicted children will become expert liars and creative manipulators. They have a keen sense of what makes you tick, what gets under your skin, and what opens your emotional heart; and they will use them all to make you believe them. A time came with our daughter when we could not even begin to understand what the truth was anymore. We so wanted to believe her when she would say she wanted to be done with the drugs and her lifestyle. When she cried and begged for our help when she was in trouble or going through withdrawal, we thought, *This is it. She will finally change.* For moments or even for months, her actions would begin to build our trust again only to be defeated by the bondage of drugs and rebellious ways. It truly was an ugly place and a horrible relationship to be in with our child. I wondered how I would ever trust my child and have a normal parent-child relationship again. Then God's still, small voice spoke to my heart. I was never to trust in man; I was only to trust in God. What an answer in the midst of a painful situation! Until my daughter trusts in God rather than mind-altering drugs, I don't have to trust her. She is living in the flesh. She is fulfilling her selfish human desires just like each one of us does when we begin to trust ourselves and men more than God.

Only God can restore our relationships with our wayward children. We can only trust Him with such a monumental task. While I may be tempted to try to fix my child, I am required to trust God with the delivery of my child from the bondage of drugs and rebellion. Even in the most difficult of situations, when I can do nothing else, I can trust that God will make good of all things for those who love Him and serve His calling according to His will. I can trust that He has this situation and that He is bigger than the problem of rebellion and drugs. He is greater than the problem of a shattered relationship with my daughter. For me, it was important to remember when I felt powerless, I can trust that God has a plan for me, a plan that is healthy and not harmful to me. Each of us, in our weakest moments, can trust that God is the Healer of all diseases including addiction and spiritual rebellion. We can trust God has conquered evil and it will not succeed forever. We should trust and believe God's ways are higher than our ways. Man will inevitably fail me because he is man and not God.

Remember this: trust God that the grief and anxiety created by failed trust between our children and us will be replaced with the peace of God. I also know that it is okay if I don't trust my child because my trust is to be placed in my Lord. He will never fail me, and He will never leave me. He will restore all things in His timing on earth and in heaven.

> *Dear Lord,*
> *Forgive my lack of trust in You when things*
> *get complicated and painful. Forgive me for*
> *placing other relationships above my relationship*
> *with You. Please replace the pain of the broken*
> *relationship I have with my child right now with*
> *Your peace and love. Thank You for continuing*

*Your work in me and Your work in my child to set
things right between us. Deliver us from the evil
placed before our family. Thank You for being all-
knowing and all-powerful in Your ways. Thank
You for being a God I can trust, believe, and
place my hope in. It is the only way I can survive
through this dark time in my life. I will put my
trust in You, God, and seek You as my refuge.*
    Amen.

Questions for Thought

~ Even though I may not trust my child, do I show
my child that no matter what I can be trusted?

~ Do I trust God? Am I able to have peace that He
knows what is best for me and that He has a plan
for me?

~ Am I going to God with my deepest needs and
desires? Am I sincere and open with Him? Am I
searching in His Word to know Him better? Am I
studying and realizing how much God truly loves
and cares for me and for the lost?

Advice from Others

> *Listen to counsel and receive instruction so that*
> *you may be wise later in life. Many plans are in a*
> *person's heart, but the LORD's decree will prevail.*
> PROVERBS 19:20–21

I tried my best to raise my children to be people of good character. As a Christian parent I also worked to instill in my children the ways of the Lord, and I strived to do my best to lead my children to the Lord. I followed advice from my parents, from child-rearing books, from my church, and the Bible.

Then I began to discover my perfect world was unraveling. I began to realize my child was straying. I realized my daughter was become increasingly rebellious. The morals and principles I worked so hard to instill in my child were becoming obsolete. I hardly recognized my child. Not only had her outward appearance changed, but her inward appearance was nothing like I thought it should have been. I ultimately discovered that my child was doing drugs. And within a few short years, my daughter had become a full-blown addict.

My mind was filled with questions. And I knew I needed to guide my child out of this evil dark place she was in. Through these trying years I have often been at a loss of what to do. Do I send her to rehab? Where is the best rehab? Do I let her stay in jail? give her another chance? trust her? Do I kick her out? On the outside the answers to these questions may seem obvious. But the love I feel for my child and the need to protect that child is overwhelming. There were times I felt blind to knowing what to do.

Let me say, my husband and I sought a lot of advice from wise counsel: godly parents, friends, counselors, pastors, doctors. It was just confusing! There were times we ignored some excellent advice, and on the flip side, we also followed some terrible advice. Ultimately, it took seeking the Lord with all our might to find the answers to know what advice to follow. Looking back, even when we followed bad advice or ignored good advice, God worked it out according to His plan. It took a little longer going our route when we did not follow God's lead, but He has been with us all along.

Being an experienced parent of an addict, I suggest seeking advice from those who are knowledgeable about addiction. It is especially wise to seek counsel from those who are not only experts about addiction but Christian as well. There are so many variables and factors to consider in the mind, body, and spirit of an addict. A person who knows nothing of addiction cannot fathom all the chemical, physical, and emotional things that are going on within the addict. Their advice, though well meant, is usually an opinion rather than good counsel.

Combining the expertise on addiction with strong Christian faith is just the icing on the cake. A Christian counselor should know that as humans we are a body, soul, and spirit. All three aspects of people are compromised by drug addiction. Their wisdom of both addiction and Christ can provide some steps for you to follow.

Being in a support group with other believers who have had similar situations lends help and wise counsel as well. It allowed me to learn about myself and others in similar circumstances. It let me know that I am not alone. I learned to let go of things I could not control and give them to God. It also brought me the unexpected joy of being able to build someone else up that was as broken as I was.

Along with seeking counsel and support, you should be in constant prayer and study His Word to find the wisdom only God can give. The Lord will provide you with the answer. You will know it is the right answer because it will align with His Word and His ways. A sense of peace will be present, and confusion will be gone. Some of the decisions will be difficult if not impossible to follow, but if it is what God is leading you to do, you must not go in any other direction!

Dear Lord,

Please give me the wisdom to make the right decisions. Lead me to wise counsel. Provide me with Your strength to follow through with the path You have led us to. Thank You for fixing what I have messed up, for guiding me as I struggle with my child, and for listening to my constant prayer. Thank You for Your Word to guide me. Allow me to be still, to block out the world's noise and hear You.

Amen.

Questions for Thought

~ Am I listening to all the advice being thrown my way, or am I choosing godly counsel?

~ Do the persons I am seeking advice from have a clear understanding of both addiction and Christianity?

~ Am I overwhelmed with advice? Do I need to fervently seek God through prayer and reading His Word? Do I need to be still and block the noise of others to hear the voice of my God?

DAY 5

Giving Your Child to God

> *"I prayed for this boy, and since the LORD gave me*
> *what I asked him for, I now give the boy to the LORD.*
> *For as long as he lives, he is given to the LORD."*
>
> 1 SAMUEL 1:27–28

I love these verses from 1 Samuel 1. It is an acknowledgment that my child's life is precious and a gift from God. I use it as a promise that as a parent I will do everything I can to teach my child about God and to raise my child in a Christian environment. The prayer above was a vow from Hannah to God for blessing her with Samuel. It shows the fulfillment of God's promise to her and reveals God's plan for Samuel to be a Levite priest. I think it is a perfect verse for parents to use as a personal praise to God for their child and a great reminder of our Christian responsibilities as parents in raising our children as God expects.

Praying this verse does not mean my child will become a priest or that my child can be saved by this verse. This verse means my child is a gift from God, and God loves my child way more than I do. God designed my child exactly as He thought best, and my responsibility is to raise my child in God's ways to the best of my abilities. God has given me a blessing, and I, in turn, make sure my child knows who God is and devote my child to God.

Proverbs 22:6 also relates to how to raise children. I am to acknowledge my responsibility as a parent so that one day as my children grow and mature, they will cling to and grasp that which is from God. It does not mean my child will be perfect—God knows mistakes will be made—but if I have been obedient to God and trained my child in His ways, then all I can do as my child becomes an adult is to trust God. I must place my child in His good hands.

When my daughter was born, she had to stay in the step-down unit for newborns for about a week for unexpected but common delivery issues. She was a fighter from the get-go and independent even as a tiny baby. God had given her a strong spirit. We had to wait several months before she could take part in the parent-child dedication at our church due to her hospitalization at birth. It was important to us that she was raised in church. We took her to church almost every Sunday. If we missed, it was because of being on vacation or illness. She took part in vacation Bible school each summer. She went to a Christian preschool. We taught her about God as much as possible.

Our daughter became a Christian at an early age. As a child she was comfortable talking about God to others. She was genuinely concerned about the salvation of others, and during her adolescent and preteen years she led several of her friends to Christ.

During her teenage years she strayed from God. She began to change friends and change interests. Looking back, those changes probably occurred because of low self-esteem from being ridiculed for being so short. That sweet spirit she had as a child became a hardened tough shield as a teenager. She was tough as nails on the outside, pretending to be invincible.

Parenting became difficult because of this tough girl rebellion. We made mistakes in our parenting during these difficult years. Our mistakes were not meant to hurt our daughter. We thought we were being godly parents and doing the right thing, but along with her self-hate, we only pushed her to be more rebellious and seek new forms of behavior to soothe and ease her pain.

Before long our daughter had become influenced by the demon of drugs and other self-destructive behaviors. Deep down she knew that what she was doing was not right in the eyes of God, and the devil used that to convince her that she had gone too far for God to forgive her. This just caused more pain and self-hatred.

We were at wit's end with what to do. My husband and I were on our knees every hour of the day praying. Our family life was out of control, and God made it obvious that we were not in control but had to give our daughter back to Him completely and give Him total control of our daughter's life. We were doing what we thought was best, but we were still not allowing God to be the focus in the midst of our troubles.

We were trying to hold on to control of our problems, to handle it ourselves because we were the parents. But my daughter needed outside help only God could provide. As we gave God control, we saw God working for the good in all our lives. Our burden was lifted, and we could hear more clearly from God. God pointed us directly to send our daughter to a Teen Challenge program five states away. This was the hardest thing I ever had to do in my life so far, but it was the way God had provided.

This verse from 1 Samuel spoke volumes to me as we sent her off to rehab. I had prayed, like Hannah, for my baby before she was born. God graciously blessed me with my daughter. My husband and I dedicated her to the Lord and sought responsibility to raise her in God's ways. She became a Christian at an early age. God had her as His child then, and He would keep hold of her no matter what happened.

I had to remember that! I had to keep in mind that she was His child forever, and He would always hold onto His sheep and run after them when they became lost. We had to give her back to Him. I prayed Proverbs 22:6 as well, laying aside any doubt of myself as a parent and remembering the good things I taught her. I had to hold on to the hope that one day she would return to God and to us.

Dear Lord,

Thank You for my child. Thank You for being dedicated forever to my child and my child to You through Your saving grace! Help me always keep You first in rearing my child, committing all my parenting ways to Your ways. Thank You for being my heavenly Father and saving me! I am a child of God! My child is a child of God!

Amen.

Additional Scripture References

Train up a child in the way he should go, even when he is old he will not depart from it. (Proverbs 22:6 NASB)

Question for Thought

~ If I have been obedient to God and taken responsibility to devote my child to God, and have acknowledged that my child is a gift from God, why am I not trusting God more with my child? Why am I holding on to my child as if I am the only one that knows the answers?

Day 6

Constant Prayer

> *Pray constantly.*
> 1 THESSALONIANS 5:17

Prayer is open communication with God. It is a time to thank God, a time to worship God, a time to repent and be forgiven by God, a time to let God know our thoughts, wants, and needs. As I grow closer to God, I have come to realize that everything needs to be done in prayer. If I act on my own without praying, I often make the wrong decisions. I have also learned to pray not only when problems arise but to pray when things are going smoothly. There have been times when things were going well, but my communication with God was at its worst. Then, when the storm came, I was at a loss of what to do and whom to talk to. If I had been in constant communication with the Lord, I would not have experienced such sheer panic.

When we have children, we are more aware of the need of prayer than ever before. Babies do not come with an instruction manual! Having a wayward child makes you fall to your knees! It took going through the painful experiences with my daughter for me to learn the importance of constant prayer. I wish I had developed a consistent prayer life before I got married and before I had children. Instead, I depended on my communication with my husband and my children to meet my emotional needs when what I needed was constant communication with Jesus through prayer to meet my spiritual needs.

Because I was not used to being in constant prayer and praying always, when my daughter began to revolt, I honestly did not know how to pray for her. I just wanted her fixed now! I was a demanding child of God. I also prayed with little faith, just saying the same prayer to God for Him to do something to stop my daughter from acting the way she was repeatedly.

There is a verse in the Bible about that kind of praying. God says those doubting prayers are like waves being blown by the wind—adrift at sea (James 1:7). Consequently, the verses preceding say, "If you don't know what you're doing, pray to the Father. He loves to help. You'll get his help, and won't be condescended to when you ask for it. Ask boldly, believingly, without a second thought" (James 1:5–6 MSG).

God heard my prayer, but I lacked faith. I believe God wanted me to mature my faith and my prayer life. As I read His Word, I saw how little faith I had. I had to believe that one day He would answer my prayer. Throughout the past few years, God has answered many of our prayers about our daughter. She is not 100 percent where we think she should be, but I know God is working both with her and our family to mature us into the Christians we are meant to be.

A believing prayer leads to peace and gives you a sense of the direction that God wants you to follow while He is working out His plan for your life. It may not be an immediate answer, but you know it is coming! It is coming in His perfect timing! So in the meantime, keep praying without any doubts. Pray without ceasing, knowing He is going to answer your prayers because He wants everyone to come to Him, and He goes after those who are lost!

When the storm comes, I will hold onto my Anchor and not let the waves toss me around with the wind, for I know He is there.

> *Dear Lord,*
> *Thank You for teaching me how to pray boldly, constantly, and without doubt! Hold me tight as I go through the storms with my child, for in the end I know You will settle us on solid ground.*
> *Amen.*

Questions for Thought

~ Am I praying for my drug-addicted child consistently and with persistence, or have I given up?

~ Am I praying boldly and without doubt, or am I doubting and just being tossed like a ship on a stormy sea?

~ Am I asking God how to pray for my child?

~ In my prayer, am I asking God to reveal my heart and make any changes in me that need to be made?

~ After I have prayed and said amen (which means "so be it"), do I acknowledge that God has heard my prayer and that He will answer my prayer in His perfect timing and in His way?

Love

> *Love never gives up. Love cares more for others than*
> *for self. Love doesn't want what it doesn't have.*
> 1 CORINTHIANS 13:4 MSG

This verse describes God's love for me! I never knew how much God loved me until I had my own children and I felt unconditional love for each of them. Nothing my children could do would change my love for them, and that is the type of love the Father has for each of us. I love the way my children look, their personalities, the sounds of their laughs, the way they love, everything about them. I love each of my children's souls and the spirits God has placed in them. However, sometimes I dislike my children. Not that I don't like them for who they are but for the way they are acting or behaving.

"To you who are ready for the truth, I say this:
Love your enemies. Let them bring out the
best in you, not the worst. When someone
gives you a hard time, respond with the ener-
gies of prayer for that person." (Luke 6:27–28
MSG)

With a rebellious child sometimes stress and frustration
cloud the unconditional love. My daughter was a rebellious
teen. She was hell-bent on having her own way no matter what
the cost or what the consequences of her behavior. Some of her
rebellious ways went against my moral compass and against
God's ways. No matter how much we punished her for her
blatant disobedience, she would often repeat the same rebellious act or display the same rebellious attitude.

Her drug use allowed the devil to have a stronghold in her
life. Her behavior, her thoughts, her actions, and her choices
were often led by her flesh-filled desires, and they were con-
trolled by the devil's trickery and lies instead of God's truths.
The drugs had control over her personality and behavior.
During these tumultuous times with my daughter, I have had
times when I disliked her. Sometimes I could not stand to be
in the same room with her, and at times I even dreaded to see
her. Then it hit me like a ton of bricks: Is this the way God
feels about me when I go against His ways and sin repeatedly?
My dislike of her behavior and choices was bringing out the
worst in me.

We all fall short. Each one of us wants our own way. We
are rebellious children in God's eyes, yet He loved us enough

that He sent His perfect Son, who never rebelled against His Father, to die for us on a cross, the punishment we each deserve for our selfish, sinful ways. God loves all mankind. He loves the sinner, and He loves the saint. I believe that when a person sins, it causes grief and pain to the heart of God. Sin creates a divide between the person and God, but our acceptance of Christ as our Savior brings us back in the same room with God; and He always wants to spend time with us. He expresses His love to us the way 1 Corinthians 13:4–8 describes because He *is* love.

My husband gave me a card with these verses on it when we got engaged, and we have tried to base our marriage on these verses. Little did I know that these same verses are excellent guidelines for the parental love of a rebellious child. God had to spell this kind of love out for us as humans because He is the only one that can love perfectly and purely in this way. We are all God's children, each of us, even in our rebellion. God loves each of us no matter what! We, in turn, can love our wayward child just as God loves us. As a challenge, place your name anywhere the word *love* is in these verses. It is a good reality check. Are you full of God's love?

I have not even come close to loving my child the way God loves me, but that does not mean I should not strive to every day. Love is a choice. It is an action, not a feeling. I choose to love no matter what a person is doing or how a person is behaving. I must love God more and more each day. I must accept God's love for me each day. I must ask God to fill me with overflowing love for others. Then, the choice to love is natural, and the actions of love are fulfilled.

I also must remember that because of the drug addiction, my child is living in the flesh, and the devil has a stronghold over her. It is not my child that I dislike. Rather, it is the devil who is my enemy, not my daughter. Luke 6:27–28 has taught me that my job right now is to love my daughter but despise the devil. I am to pray for my daughter and in the name of Jesus rebuke the devil from her life, all with a childlike faith from me. I am still learning this one, but the more I lean on Christ, pray without ceasing, keep my thoughts and heart pure, and guard my tongue, the easier it is to have faith for what I cannot see or control, and to fight the devil! I cannot have any doubts whatsoever! I must ask the Lord to fill me with His love and grace so they overflow from me to my daughter. I must love her through the eyes and heart of Christ. No matter her choices and actions, I must allow God to bring out the best in me and not display my worst toward her. Otherwise, how else will my daughter truly know the love of Christ?

> *Dear Lord,*
> *Thank You that You are love! Please forgive*
> *my inadequate love for others and my child.*
> *Thank You for reminding me that I am just*
> *as rebellious as my child is. Forgive me that I*
> *want my way all the time. Forgive my rebellious*
> *nature. Thank You, Lord, for helping me realize*
> *it is not my child that I dislike; it is the devil who*
> *is seeking to destroy my family and weaken our*
> *faith. Thank You that You are the ultimate victor!*

*When times get difficult, remind me who my true
enemy is and help me respond with prayer over
my child. I am more than a conqueror through
Christ Jesus who strengthens me. Lord Jesus, fill
me with Your abundant love and grace so they
overflow toward others no matter how others
may act or behave toward me. I love You, Lord,
and I accept that You love me no matter what.
Please overflow me with Your love that I may
love unconditionally as You do.*

   Amen.

Additional Scripture References

Love doesn't strut, doesn't have a swelled
head, doesn't force itself on others, isn't always
"me first," doesn't fly off the handle, doesn't
keep score of the sins of others, doesn't revel
when others grovel, takes pleasure in the
flowering of truth, puts up with anything,
trusts God always, always looks for the best,
never looks back, but keeps going to the end.
(1 Corinthians 13:4–7 MSG)

Questions for Thought

~ Do I truly know how much God loves me?

~ Am I basing my love for God, my child, and myself on feelings and emotions, or am I basing my love from God's perspective—unconditionally and through choice and obedient action?

~ Do I recognize who the true enemy is in this battle with addiction?

~ Are my child's behavior and choices bringing out the best in me or the worst in me?

~ While I hate the evil of drugs and I will take a stand against this evil, is my child seeing that my love will never give up and my love for my child is unconditional? Or am I showing judgment, selfishness, anger, impatience, and unforgiveness?

PART II

Throwing in the Anchor

You have prepared your ship against the wind, waves, and rain that come with a child bound by addiction by becoming as one in your marriage—by trusting only God, seeking wise counsel, giving your child to God, praying without ceasing, and learning to love unconditionally. Now you are ready to throw in the anchor. With the release of the anchor, you are letting go of some baggage you are carrying and ridding yourself of the lies of the enemy so that once the anchor has reached its Rock, you shall not be moved as you battle the storm of addiction with your child.

Anger

In your anger do not sin. Do not let the sun go down while
you are still angry, and do not give the devil a foothold.
EPHESIANS 4:26–27 NIV

Anger is a tremendous emotion often expelled on a rebellious child. I used to think being angry was a sin. Though rarely, anger is an emotion God expresses in the Bible. Jesus even knew this emotion. I am made in His image, so anger is an emotion I feel as well. If you are angry, this is not a sin. The key is not to sin in our anger—to get over it and forgive those who made you angry.

As a parent with a wayward child, I did not handle anger well. To be candid, I sinned numerous times in my anger. It usually takes me awhile to get angry unless I am tired or stressed, but a child addicted to drugs will make you both tired and stressed, so over the last few years I have been angry often. At times I was so angry at my child I not only thought bad things, but they came out of my mouth! Thankfully God convicted me of my sin, and I sought forgiveness from Him and from my child. Notice God did not condemn me. Unfortunately, some of those times took several days for me to ask forgiveness because I thought I was justified in my anger. I mean who wouldn't be angry and have a raging fit when your drug-addicted child repeatedly disobeys, blatantly disrespects you by screaming profanities at you and other family members, or even shows violent behavior toward you or your property.

My husband and I disciplined our child for exhibiting those behaviors. She was often grounded, stripped of her cell phone, lost driving privileges, and sometimes everything was taken away. The punishment was justified and an expected duty as a parent. But my own fits of rage that resulted in using profanity or name calling of my child were not justified! I was sinning in my anger. I gave the devil a foothold and was being myself a rebellious child of God.

To be even more candid, I let my anger build up as resentment toward my child. I believed I did nothing to deserve this upheaval that was occurring in my household, and I let my anger fester. At one point my anger had taken such control over me, I would resent people who seemed to have perfect children. In fact, I would get angry at people trying to give advice because I didn't think they could understand what I was going through. I would get mad at my other child for no good reason just because I let that anger get out of control. I even got angry with God at times and would go for days without praying or reading my daily devotions. Sometimes I did not even go to church. What a foothold I had given to the devil.

As a family we went to counseling for reasons related to our daughter's drug use. During counseling we learned how to manage all the anger that was being expressed, but it took God's getting my attention and convicting me of my sin. Graciously He did not pour out His wrath on me like I deserved. He forgave me of my sin of mishandling my anger. I asked for forgiveness from my child for sinning in my anger, and I forgave my child for what was making me angry. I am still not perfect or where I hope to be one day with dealing with anger, but I am trying to be slower to anger. I read my Bible often to hear what God has to say about anger. God revealed that I was never meant to harbor anger. I needed to give it to Him. He had to show me who I was fighting against.

One of my favorite passages about anger comes from Ephesians 4:26–27. This is one to follow precisely because sinning in anger has consequences that are very painful. Letting anger manifest into sin is like allowing cancer into the soul. It is best to let your child know you are angry and why you are angry. Speak truth over the situation. Show grace just as Christ does with us. There may be just cause to discipline a child or consequences warranted if the child has done something wrong, but remember your goal is to teach and guide to promote better behavior—not punish out of anger. Settle the cause of the anger and let the anger go before you sleep because the devil will have a foothold. Not that anger about a wayward child is bad; it is not ours to hold on to because it will manifest into sin. Our anger is real, but God must be the one to take that emotion and be the One who manages this emotion in our life, not us! Ask God to replace your anger with peace and love that only He can do when you are angry.

> *Dear Lord,*
> *Thank You that it is okay to be angry. But Lord, please do not let me sin in my anger. Please fill me with love and compassion toward my child, even when I am angry. Help me be slow to anger. Help me give my anger to You and forgive quickly before the sun goes down. Keep the devil away when anger is felt. Give us Your wisdom in dealing with our anger toward our own child. Help me speak truth with grace.*
> *Amen.*

Questions for Thought

~ Do I sin against my child and others because of anger about my child's drug use?

~ Does God lash out in anger against me, or does He speak truth with grace, convict but not condemn to promote repentance or turning from my sin? Do I show the same godly anger toward my child?

~ Do I release my anger to God and allow healing and peace within my soul so that the devil does not have a foothold in me? Or do I choose to hang on to my anger, let it fester, allow bitterness and rage to consume me so that I am not only sinning against others but also against God?

~ Once I lay down my anger and give it to God, do I ask God to fill me with His peace and wisdom?

Guilt

> *Guilt is banished through love and truth;*
> *Fear-of-God deflects evil.*
> PROVERBS 16:6 MSG

I am guilty of sinning as a parent and have known guilt even after I confessed my sin to God, knowing He forgave my sin. If you have ever dealt with a child who has done something for the hundredth time, you know the emotion of total rage and frustration. Maybe you degraded your child as a person or made your child feel making things right again would come at a cost or even neglected to discipline your child out of pure exhaustion. This is the reality of parenting a child addicted to drugs. I am guilty and at times have even felt that it is my fault my daughter behaves as she does and uses drugs because of my failures as a parent.

Thankfully, Christ died for my sin, and when I cry out for forgiveness, my God forgives me. Proverbs 16:6 says that guilt is removed through love and truth. God is love, and God is truth. When we accept Jesus as our Savior, confess our sin and seek forgiveness, our transgressions are removed, and our relationship with Him is restored. Hence we are no longer guilty. We may have some consequences to deal with and earthly relationships to repair, but God has wiped the slate clean.

So if God has forgiven my sins in parenting and given me a fresh start, why do I sense so much guilt? I feel guilty for even trying to write this devotional. Who am I to do this? My child is a drug addict. What type of parent am I? I am not a Bible scholar or a preacher. I keep making stupid mistakes. If I am forgiven and my sin is forgotten, why do I feel this way? By reading God's Word, I realize that my guilt is from not forgiving myself, and my guilt is from the devil. He wants to steal my joy.

I must forgive myself for the mistakes I have made and quit wallowing in self-pity and selfish guilt-driven thoughts. These thoughts and feelings are not from God. They are from the devil, the master of lies, the deceiver of truth, the one who seeks to destroy my family and steal my peace. The second half of Proverbs 16:6 that "fear-of-God deflects evil." To be God-fearing, I must stay in God's Word often to learn how He parents me. I must place Him first above even my rebellious child.

I must totally give my problems over to God and let Him have control. I must ask and seek His wisdom to be a better parent. I must turn a deaf ear to the devil and listen to God's Word. I must acknowledge that I am a sinner saved by grace through Jesus Christ and that my sins of the past, present, and future are forgiven when I confess my sin. I must seek His forgiveness every day of my existence to keep me from hiding in my own shame. Jesus Christ dealt with my sins once and for all with His own precious life on the cross.

I would be guilty if I had unconfessed sin. I would be guilty if I refused to accept Christ as my Savior. Guilt is a burden we have when we have sinned. I should confess my sins to God and seek His forgiveness. If I have sinned against someone, I should ask for forgiveness. Once I have repented of these things, I should remember that I am free and right before God's eyes. Any further feelings of guilt are from the devil and should be driven away in God's name! For the Lord Jesus Christ does not condemn. He provides only conviction that turns me from my sin, draws me closer to Him, and in the end makes me more like Him.

> *Dear Lord,*
> *Please forgive my sin and make me white as snow. Please forgive my poor parenting skills and lack of wisdom I have with my child. Restore my relationship with my child. Please remove my guilt and replace it with Your peace and Your love. Grant me wisdom in raising my child. Help me remember how You parent me. Keep the devil away and don't let me listen to his lies. Thank You for sending Your Son, Jesus, to take away our sin and restore us to You.*
> *Amen.*

Questions for Thought

~ Am I allowing guilt to consume who I am? Do I truly understand how God sees me?

~ Have I totally accepted His forgiveness of my sin? Have I forgiven myself as God has forgiven me?

~ Do I realize that if I harbor guilt, I will hide in shame and never be an effective parent?

Forgiveness

> *Then Peter approached him and asked, "Lord, how many*
> *times shall I forgive my brother or sister who sins against*
> *me? As many as seven times?" "I tell you, not as many*
> *as seven," Jesus replied, "but seventy times seven."*
>
> MATTHEW 18:21–22

Sin has a domino effect. Sin does not just affect the person sinning; it affects everyone that person knows and has a relationship with.

During the last several years, I had to ask God to help me forgive:

- My child: Her choices, disobedience, lies, deceit, disrespect, attitude, and the pain created in my life and my family's life

- Her friends: Their lack of wisdom, choices, judgment, disobedience, lies, dishonesty, and deceitfulness in hiding what was going on with my daughter
- Her school: Their failure to guide my child, their lack of following through with agreements made in parental meetings, teachers just "working a job" and lack of genuine care for an individual, their laziness in fulfilling their responsibilities as educators, counselors, and administrators
- My friends: My real friends have spent time with me, listened, and have prayed daily for my daughter and my family, but I needed to forgive my social or acquaintance friends for not telling me what was going on or what they suspected until it was too late, and afterward for their complete withdrawal from me and my daughter. I felt betrayed and like an outcast. I could see the discomfort in their faces if they saw me anywhere. Unfortunately, with drug addiction, people don't know how to approach you. It is viewed by human eyes as a willful sin of the addict. People also judge your skills as a parent. While out in public I often heard people talk or express concern about other children sick with a disease. It would hurt

because in my case some people did not know how to communicate about my daughter's addiction. Instead of stopping to ask about my daughter or our situation, a few friends would just avoid me when they saw me in a public setting.

- My husband: As he was dealing with his own pain, I felt neglected at times. As he was dealing with his own anger, I felt like he was angry with me.

- My family: My family members are wonderful, godly people, and they have really helped during this trial in our lives. But sometimes opinions were expressed, body language and comments were made that cut to the my core as a person and a parent. My son loves his sister and is truly a wonderful Christian young man, but sometimes I could just see the anger and dislike he had for his sister. Sometimes he would try to be disobedient just because "she" was getting away with everything.

- My church: My true friends and church family—the ones that love unconditionally and forgive everything and do not judge, do not gossip or spread rumors—I cherish forever. However, some of the people in my church, especially in my daughter's peer group, judged my daughter. They pushed her away from God and saw my daughter's sins and problems without removing the "log" in their own eyes. Many excluded my daughter and looked at her with "haughty" eyes.

- Myself: For somehow failing to meet the needs my daughter was seeking and for being too busy to listen to my daughter. I needed to forgive myself for always having time to give an opinion or throw "the Christian" way of doing things in her face, which only drove her farther from God. As difficult as it is, I needed to forgive myself for being so angry at the world—angry at God, my family, my husband, and totally disliking the people who led my daughter astray or the ones that allowed my daughter to go astray by being silent. I needed to forgive myself for not liking my daughter at times, for not living wholly for God even in the troubled times, for allowing the devil any room to do his dirty work, for being a selfish daughter, daughter-in-law, wife, and parent, and for not being the Christian example.

In all the sin that was going on in our lives and our tiny world, I could hear God's still, small voice speaking, "Forgive them, for they know not what they do!" (see Luke 23:34). I remembered all the things Christ had forgiven me of personally in the past. I knew the only way to begin to heal was to forgive the people who directly or indirectly caused my pain. I knew that I was full of the world's ways and not God's ways by hanging onto my unforgiveness of others and myself. I have learned the following about forgiveness: Forgiveness is not making light of the offense. Forgiveness is not forgetting what happened. Forgiveness is not reconciliation. Forgiveness is a choice. When I forgave, I was no longer held captive by the offense. When I forgave, I could allow God to heal my heart so that my memory would be without pain and anger. When I forgave, I was freed; my enemies could no longer hold me prisoner. Some relationships have been reconciled while other relationships have become more of a season of my life with no hard feelings and no regret.

It was incredible to feel the weight of the albatross I had hung around my neck lifted when I asked God to help me forgive every person. Notice that I had to ask for help to forgive. Asking for forgiveness was difficult, but once done, I realized how much time I had wasted just hanging on to all that sinful baggage! Forgiveness is not about others really. It is about being obedient to God, following in His footsteps. Forgiveness allows me to be a whole person devoted to God. It allows my heart to heal and grow. It strengthens my own personal faith because I realize how much I have been forgiven by God and His amazing sacrifice of His Son in forgiving each of my sins.

Dear Lord,

I think in this whole ordeal forgiveness was the hardest lesson for me to learn. Yet it was the most crucial for me to understand and to obey. Thank You that You are the source of forgiveness and that I don't have to rely on my own personal strength and heart to forgive. Thank You for sending Christ to save me from my sins! Thank You for forgiving me!

Amen.

Questions for Thought

~ Who do I need to forgive?

~ Have I forgiven myself?

~ Have I completely accepted God's forgiveness, or do I feel the need to crucify Christ repeatedly?

~ Do I understand what forgiveness is about, and will I allow God to help me forgive others and myself?

Fear

> *"So do not fear, for I am with you; do not be dismayed,*
> *for I am your God. I will strengthen you and help you;*
> *I will uphold you with my righteous right hand."*
>
> ISAIAH 41:10 NIV

Each one of us has something or someone that makes us fearful. Each one of us may react differently to fear based on our own personalities and character. Fear can be good when used to protect us from dangerous situations, but fear can also be bad, especially when it keeps us from doing God's will or causes us not to rely on God when things get a little scary.

Fear tends to gets my heart racing, increases my respiratory rate, causes nausea/vomiting, headaches, breaks me out into a cold sweat, and makes me want to run, escape, or hide. It can cause me to be hostile and angry. It may cause me to scream

or cry. The physical and psychological effects of fear are terrible. If faced with danger like a wild animal or a falling heavy
object, I instinctively run. God gave me that as common sense.
However, I do not think God wants me to have irrational fears
or to fear what life here on earth may present me with.

Things I have feared having a drug-addicted child include:
rejection from friends, family, even my daughter, failure of my
marriage, that my son will turn out the same as my daughter,
over our finances being too exhausted to help my daughter, for
my health and loved ones' health due to the stress of the situation, and that my daughter's actions and addictions will either
kill her or someone else. I have feared that this problem will
never end—that I am stuck with this problem until I die! For
me fear does not go well because I also happen to be a worrier.
The two are a bad combination. With four years of worrying
about my child and the related fears, I should be crazier than
I am, or I should be dead from physical and psychological
ramifications.

Thankfully, by the grace of God, when I fear, He whispers, "Do not be afraid, for I am with you. I will never forsake
you or leave you." I find it funny and even maddening at times
that He never says the problem will go away. He promises to
be our strength and carry us when we cannot handle any more
fear and challenges. I firmly believe God is in the miracle
business and that He can do anything to change the situation.
I also know beyond a shadow of a doubt that if my situation
never changes He will remain the same. Therefore, I shouldn't
be afraid. I guess I am like Peter when he walked on water
with Jesus. For a moment he had no fear but let his faith in

God lead him through an impossible feat. But when he relied on himself and took his eyes off Christ, he became fearful; he doubted, and he sank. Fortunately, God never changes. He keeps on loving and believing in you and me as He did Peter. He kept sustaining Peter in difficulties and eventually carried him home to glory, as He will do for you and me.

To combat fear, I must keep my eyes on Jesus. Additionally, I must not make my fears bigger than my God. I must take captive my thoughts and feelings and remember God's Word and His promises. I must accept that God will be with me even when I walk in the valley. I must grasp because of what Christ did on the cross that I am eternally protected, and my child is eternally protected.

One day I will grow into a fearless woman of God. God's not done with me yet! And I have a lot of spiritual growing to do. My prayer is that if you are a parent out there and you are experiencing these same fears, you will let God be your Hero and your Savior. I pray that you will face the problems and concerns with a firm foundation that God is carrying you and upholding you with His hand.

> *Dear Lord,*
> *I ask that You remove fear from me in Jesus name. Be my strength and uphold me when I can't see past my fears. Let me see and feel Your presence. Hold me when I am shaking and frozen with fear. Sustain and strengthen me. Send peace*

and give me eternal perspective. Thank You that
nothing can ever separate You from me.
    Amen.

Questions for Thought

~ What do I fear the most in this battle of addiction with my child?

~ What does God say about fear? Have I looked in the Bible at all the verses about fear and let them settle over me?

~ Can I let go of my fear and give it to God to handle? Will I allow God to strengthen me and uphold me by submitting my fear?

~ As a child of God, do I acknowledge that nothing can separate me from God? That this present world is only a vapor, my home is in heaven, and God has already won the battle? Or, that even if the worst happens, God will always be here with me until He calls me home to heaven? Or, that God has a place for me and my child in heaven? Do I have this eternal perspective to focus on when everything else here seems so scary?

DAY 12

Strength

> *It is strength that endures the unendurable and spills over into joy, thanking the Father who makes us strong enough to take part in everything bright and beautiful that he has for us.*
> COLOSSIANS 1:12 MSG

Human strength increases when we actively use our muscles in a way that combines power, force, and adequate load. If effort is continuously put in, strength will increase. Our bodies will find the most efficient way to perform a task; therefore, once in a strength training program, it is easy to plateau if we do the same training day after day. A good strength program allows for muscle confusion to provide growth and gains. Thus, a variety of movements, loads at different angles, and speed help produce strong muscles. But what about our emotional and spiritual strength? How do we get stronger in these areas of our life?

Our Father in heaven tells us many times in His Word He is the source of our strength. The Bible also states God's strength "comes into its own in your weakness" (2 Cor. 12:9–10 MSG). Like strength training, spiritual strength comes with consistent effort, which is time spent in our relationship with Christ. In physical strengthening we are usually to some extent in control of our growth and progression (although some feats of physical strength can only be explained by God). On the other hand, with spiritual strengthening we are not in control; we have no strength on our own—we are weak. The only tool we have to strengthen ourselves is the utter and complete submission of ourselves and our situation to Christ, our Lord. That submission also includes a complete focus on Christ, obedience to His Word, and His direction. Similar to physical strengthening, spiritual strengthening can be anguishing, produce pain, cause you to fall on your face, and cause opposition in our human realm. It can come at you in many forms and allows no room for a plateau. It can hit you from any angle and confuse the heck out of you. Thankfully, just as physical training produces outward and inward effects, spiritual strengthening reveals God's glory inside and out. Spiritual strengthening allows us to become more like Christ.

Loving a drug addict made me realize I was weak, not only physically and mentally but also spiritually. I tried to handle everything myself. If only I could be the perfect parent, discipline more, be a better example, be a better leader, be a better advisor, be more understanding, be tougher, be stronger, then I could make my child behave as she should, and I could make her stop using drugs. Even though I was using various parenting skills, angles, strategies, and force, I could not handle the burden of raising an addicted child. Temporary relief came when my husband and I invested time with various trainers such as grandparents, Christian friends, our pastor, and even medical and psychological professionals. We gained strength from the use of these sources, and some of what they suggested worked, but these ultimately failed to fuel our strength in the long run. God had to become our strength in our weakness! My husband and I had to surrender everything, including our daughter, to Him.

With my daughter's drug addiction, I was brought to my knees! One of our most fearful times occurred when my daughter had been caught again with drugs and arrested by the police. We, as a family, including my daughter (in a round-about way) agreed—through God's heavy direction—she had to leave home and attend a Christian intervention program for teens. I was so scared. I understood how Abraham must have felt when God asked him to sacrifice his only son or the way Samson felt when the one he loved cut off his source of strength! I was weak. I didn't think I could handle it. How can a father have the strength to fly thousands of miles away from home with his daughter and just leave her there with strangers? How can a mother stand to watch her child go without knowing if she will ever come back? How can a married couple sustain "the love of their love" being gone? How can parents be strong for their other child while that sibling is at a loss for his big sister?

The Lord showed me the answer in Colossians 1:12. God was my source of strength as I submitted and relied on

Him. Even though our physical and emotional weaknesses in this world may never change, God's glory will ultimately triumph, and spiritual strength can increase. Spiritual strength will flourish when consistent prayer and time spent focusing on Christ instead of heartache, pain, failures, and weakness becoming your "personal trainer." Remember to look for God in the midst of suffering. He may come in simple ways such as "thinking of you" cards in the mail, "how are you doing?" phone calls or texts, or plainly written words only God meant you to see. God reached out to us on my husband's way to the Christian intervention program for teens. My husband and I were so worried about whether we were doing the right thing. While on the bus taking my daughter to her destination, my husband noticed a sign over the bus driver's head. The sign read: "Your courtesy driver today is Jesus!" Hallelujah! It was a simple sign—actually the name of the bus driver—but to us, it was God's way of showing up at our weakest moment. God had just provided us with the strength to leave our daughter in His hands and the hands of Christian strangers.

Just as building human strength takes time, so does building spiritual strength. It cannot be done overnight or in just a few weeks—it takes a lifetime. But my heavenly Father is my Source of strength, and He will conquer all my weaknesses! He will provide me with strength, and He will sustain me through this battle with drug addiction. He will help me endure the unendurable. His power and control will be delivered as I submit everything to Him. He will bless me with a strong spirit full of joy and thankfulness in an otherwise impossible situation.

Dear Lord,

Thank You for being my source of strength. Thank You for the strength to breathe in and out! Thank You for being here. Thank You for silencing my fears! Thank You for letting me yell and cry and then pulling me out of the pit! Forgive me when I lose my focus on You and have a pity party or a panic attack instead. Thank You for Christian family and friends You send to help keep me strong. Thank You for being so obvious when I am blind. Thank You for who You are. Thank You for showing up! Thank You that even though the physical pain and sadness of my weakness are present, Your strength gives me power and joy for the future You control!

Amen.

Questions for Thought

~ Do I depend on my strength to fight the battle of addiction with my child, or am I relying on God as my source of strength?

~ Am I strong spiritually?

~ How can I improve my spiritual strength and ignore the weakness I feel physically, mentally, and emotionally?

Spiritual Warfare

> *Elisha said, "Don't be afraid, for those who are with us*
> *outnumber those who are with them." Then Elisha prayed,*
> *"LORD, please open his eyes and let him see." So the LORD*
> *opened the servant's eyes, and he saw that the mountain was*
> *covered with horses and chariots of fire all around Elisha.*
> 2 KINGS 6:16–17

I had heard of spiritual warfare but never experienced it until my daughter hit the age of sixteen and her drug issue reached a fever pitch. Time has passed, and as much as I hate it, our family is still in the midst of spiritual warfare. I guess everyone is in the middle of spiritual warfare, whether it is a battle with drugs, alcohol, finances, disease, or whatever the devil is doing here on earth to hold onto the lost and steal joy and create doubt in the faith of Christians.

Over the last four years, we have had tough battles with my daughter's rebellious nature and her addiction to drugs. We have had some victories over these issues—times of peace and joy and times when everything in the world was right (a little heaven on earth). But the devil is still prowling, waiting for when we are weak or comfortable and he's ready to pounce, to engage in battle again!

Revelation 12:4 says, "The Dragon crouched before the Woman in childbirth, poised to eat up the Child when it came" (MSG). The devil is in an all-out war with God. He is here on earth trying his best to recruit to his army and destroy those who are of God. He is trying his best to kill our daughter with drugs and with a rebellious spirit. She is a Christian, but she is in bondage because of the drugs. She is full of shame, pain, and self-loathing, and it has made her faith weak.

She has attempted to give this stronghold over to God, but this sin, this god of her life, the devil, keeps throwing her way, grabbing her every time. She has brief periods of victory over evil, but I think she is a lot like Elisha's servant in 2 Kings. She has little faith and can't see the angel armies surrounding her. She has forgotten to wear the armor of God. In her drug-addicted mind, she feels unworthy of anything God would have for her.

Likewise, we have been blind to "the mountainside full of horses and chariots of fire surrounding" (2 Kings 6:17 MSG) us. Instead, we believe the devil's lies that we are fighting alone in a no-win situation. Unfortunately, we also have been found unprepared for the battle in front of us—found with no weapons or protection. I have let my body and my soul—my mind, will, and emotions—grow louder than the Holy Spirit within me. Watching my child suffer drug addiction causes pain both physically and emotionally within me. Fear of the unknown overtakes me. Doubt drowns me.

Ephesians 6:10 speaks about the armor of God. We are to shield ourselves with truth, righteousness, peace, faith, and salvation. We are to apply them, not just hear the words. I have applied salvation, truth, and righteousness, but I keep forgetting to fasten faith and peace to myself. These two parts seem to keep falling off. Instead I wear doubt and fear.

I am listening to the lies of the devil. But God calls me to be a mighty warrior for Him. This same chapter of Ephesians states God's Word is an indispensable weapon, and prayer is essential in this never-ending battle. I must learn to grab these weapons first instead of relying on myself when the devil attacks.

Even though God has the ultimate victory, we still have our battle responsibilities. God has given us everything we need to fight *from* victory not *to* victory. One of our biggest responsibilities in this spiritual warfare is to take every thought captive and align it with the Word of God. Spending time daily with God and studying His Word provide such a strong fortress for a parent of a drug addict. Do not listen to what the devil says or let your feelings overwhelm you. Seize and use the weapon of prayer. Pray without doubt and claim God's promises through Scripture over every situation this demon of drug addiction throws at you. Realize angel armies surround you, and they outnumber those of the enemy.

I am learning to be a mighty warrior for God, and I hope my daughter will learn to be the same. I pray she will quit letting the devil hold her as a prisoner of war because she is not his; she is a child of God. I know ultimately the battle will be won and His glory and power will reign forever. In the meantime I have only to take my marching orders and to obey my Commanding Officer, for He is the victor! He is in control! He will not be defeated!

> *Dear Lord,*
>
> *I ask You to forgive me for not being prepared for battle. I ask You to forgive me for retreating or going AWOL in this war I seem unable to win. I ask You to keep me centered and focused on You, Your word, and always connected with prayer. I ask that when I doubt or am afraid You will show me Your strength. I ask You to prepare me before the trouble comes so I will still be standing when it is passed. Remind me to take my thoughts captive and to align my defense to Your Word and promises. Thank You for having the final say in this world and victory over evil.*
>
> *Amen.*

Additional Scripture References

> For this reason take up the full armor of God, so that you may be able to resist in the evil day, and having prepared everything, to take your stand. (Ephesians 6:13)

Questions for Thought

~ Am I applying the armor of God to myself each day—all of it, not parts and pieces?

~ Do I acknowledge God as the ultimate Victor, that He is fighting my battles and surrounds me with His angel armies?

~ Do I see the spiritual warfare in this world for what it is? Am I a mighty warrior armed with God's Word and constant prayer?

~ Do I cast off fear and doubt? Do I take my thoughts captive and align them with God's Word and promises?

DAY 14

Worry and Anxiety

Don't worry about anything, but in everything, through prayer and petition with thanksgiving, present your requests to God. And the peace of God, which surpasses all understanding, will guard your hearts and minds in Christ Jesus.

PHILIPPIANS 4:6–7

I am by nature a worrier. I worry about everything. Luckily, God gave me a husband that handles worrying beautifully, and my husband has helped to balance my tendencies. If God had not worked on my worrying and continued to use my husband to help me through it, with all that has come with our wayward child and the shackles of addiction, I would be insane right now.

Proverbs 12:25 says worry weighs us down. Before long, worrisome thoughts become irrational thoughts and manifest themselves into physical symptoms of sickness and disease.

Things I have worried about over my child have included:

~ What if she dies?

~ What if she gets arrested?

~ What if she refuses treatment?

~ What if she gets an illness because of her drug addiction?

~ What if we run out of money trying to help her?

~ What if my marriage doesn't survive this ordeal?

~ What if she doesn't get better?

~ What if my family thinks we are wrong in our approach to help our daughter?

And the list goes on.

The funny thing is some of what I worried about happened. She was arrested several times. She got illnesses from her risky behavior. We nearly lost all our financial means in trying to help her recover. And she is not any better—I worried for nothing. These things happened, but God helped my family and me through each one of them. The worrying was a waste. What I should have been doing more of was praying. I prayed, but I worried more.

I still worry about some of the other things on my list, especially about what if she dies? But as soon as the thought comes to my mind, I focus on God. I know He loves her far more than I do, and He will do what is best for her. My husband and I have come to terms with her possible death. Not all things end the way we want them to, but we have decided God will get the glory even through her death if that were to happen. We will not let the devil and the evil he has thrown at our family win. That determination is a worry stopper for sure. The battle is won no matter what!

The worst things I worry about may come true, or they may not. Either way, God deserves the glory because He will be there to walk through the fire with me. He will rescue me from defeat. He is greater than my worst worry and greatest fear. He is writing the story, and it will eventually end well, even if it differs significantly from what I envisioned.

Having a child or loved one who is an addict is no fun. Addicts never know the turmoil they are causing in other people's lives. God knows the turmoil I am experiencing though, and He does not want my life to be consumed with anxiousness and fear. He wants me to know and believe in Him, to trust Him no matter what the outcome may be. I am to cast my fears and anxious thoughts onto Him. I am to ask Him to fill me with His power, strength, and peace. I am to call upon His name when anxious thoughts overtake me, give praise unto Him that delivers me and gives me supernatural strength!

To drop to my knees before the Lord, to give Him praise and let my petitions be known to Him is the way to go. He will displace the worry. He will replace it with His goodness, His mercy, and His peace. My circumstance may not change, but He is the Victor over evil. He will fight our battles right alongside me and will carry me when I can no longer fight. Worry not! Pray more! Seek the presence of the Lord.

> *Dear Lord,*
> *Forgive my worrying. Call me to you when I worry. Turn my mind and heart toward You. I will praise You when I fear and turn my petitions to Your ear. Thank You for hearing me and for turning my worry into focus on You. You are working for my good. Things may or may not happen. My job is to stay focused on You and not the what-ifs.*
> *Amen.*

Additional Scripture References

> "But seek first the kingdom of God and his righteousness, and all these things will be provided for you. Therefore don't worry about tomorrow, because tomorrow will worry about itself. Each day has enough trouble of its own." (Matthew 6:33–34)

Questions for Thought

~ When I worry, do I realize I am belittling my faith and not trusting God?

~ If I am not willing to submit my problems to God, am I capable of taking responsibility for everything drug addiction will throw my way? If I am not capable of handling it, why can't I give it to the One who is capable of handling it?

~ How is my fretting over a situation going to change the circumstance? If I can do something to help, am I seeking God for wisdom and being active in His strength to carry out the task? If it is an issue I have no control over, why do I persist in carrying the burden? Who can carry the weight?

Day 15

Sleeplessness

*If I'm sleepless at midnight, I spend the hours in
grateful reflection. Because you've always stood up
for me, I'm free to run and play. I hold onto you
for dear life and you hold me steady as a post.*
PSALM 63:6–8 MSG

The trials I have been through with my daughter over the
last few years have caused me to lose a lot of sleep. Bad
habits such as worrying, replaying arguments in my mind, and
overthinking have caused me to develop full-blown insomnia.
I have gone days—sometimes four or five in a row—without
sleeping more than an hour or two each night. I have dreaded
nightfall because I knew I would be miserable again and
unable to sleep.

The lack of sleep caused me to develop anxiety and depression, have mood swings, lack energy, be unable to form clear thoughts, and forget things I would normally remember. I was always sick, and my body was out of a natural rhythm. I was so miserable I eventually went to the doctor about my insomnia; he put me on medicine because of the unhealthy state I was in physically and emotionally.

The medicine helped for a while, but I knew I did not want to be on it forever. While it had restored my sleep pattern and I could function again as a human, a wife, a mom, and as an employee, as soon as I tried to come off the medication, something would happen with my daughter that would force me back to a place of dependence.

It was becoming a crutch I no longer wanted with me! After two years of trying to stop taking the sleep medicine, God got my attention during a twenty-one-day prayer and fasting event we had at our church. God showed me that the things that were causing me to lose sleep were also taking my focus off of Him.

I was worrying, thinking negatively, hanging on to anger, holding onto fear and doubt, and not surrendering everything to Him. I knew each of these was wrong, and I was not walking my talk. I was not living out my faith and beliefs. I was thinking about having faith, I was talking about having faith, but I was not acting on faith the way God wanted me to. He wanted me to surrender everything, including what I was thinking about at night, and He wanted me to give the dreams that would jolt me awake to Him.

During the twenty-one days of prayer and fasting, I learned I had to cling to God. I replaced my thoughts and desires with His thoughts and desires. I replaced worry with trust. I replaced anger with forgiveness. I replaced fear and doubt with peace and conquered victory. I replaced negative thinking with thanksgiving. At the end of the twenty-one days, God showed me through depending on Him in my weakness He could accomplish what needed to be done. My initial desire during the prayer and fasting was to see a change in my daughter, but by the end of the twenty-one days, God showed me I needed to change some things in my life.

My daughter's rebellion and addiction remained unchanged for a reason only God knows. Remarkably, I could change and live by faith; I could sleep. I still do not get perfect rest, but it is nothing like the horrible insomnia I experienced. I still get those human thoughts of worry and anger at night that try to keep me up, but now instead of dwelling on them, I pray to God. I meditate on the goodness of God. I worship Him in my sleeplessness, and before I know it, I am resting peacefully in His loving arms in the midst of the pain.

> *Dear Lord,*
> *Thank You for using the twenty-one days of prayer and fasting to change me. Thank You for showing me how staying close to You and giving everything to You will bring me rest even though the circumstances may not change. Thank You that I can spend time with You when I am restless and*

cannot sleep. Thank You that in Your presence I
can find rest.
    Amen.

Questions for Thought

~ What is causing my sleeplessness? Worry? Fear?
  My own irrational thoughts?

~ What good is it doing me to lie in bed and hang
  on to these "sleep stealers"? Have I gotten up and
  engaged God with my sleeplessness?

~ Am I resting in His presence, or am I consumed
  with my own thoughts?

DAY 16

Pain and Suffering

> *"What did I do to deserve this? Did I ever hit anyone
> who was calling for help? Haven't I wept for those
> who live a hard life, been heartsick over the lot of the
> poor? But where did it get me? I expected good but evil
> showed up. I looked for light but darkness fell."*
>
> JOB 30:24–26 MSG

Job was a good man and he loved God. At one point he
had it all—friends, good family, health, and wealth. But
Job was not perfect, and neither was his family. Job made
sacrificial atonements not only for his personal sins but also for
the sins of his family. He was obedient to God and tried his
best to follow God's ways. Yet he lost everything. He lost his
children, his wealth, his health, and his influence in society.

Now I have not had it as bad as Job, but I have suffered, and I understand to a degree where Job is coming from. I lost the child I once knew to drugs. Friends abandoned me. I was shunned by people in public places because I was the parent of an addict. I have been physically and mentally sick from the sheer exhaustion of trying to parent a drug-abusing child. I have been put under financial strain. I experienced anguish and pain.

I have experienced suffering I did not understand. It would feel just to have this pain if I had been a bad person or committed some terrible act. I am by no means perfect and without sin, but when I sin or realize I have sinned, I ask for forgiveness as quickly as possible. I try to do what is right. So I, like Job, asked God, "Why, God? Why did this happen? Haven't I been good and done what You asked of me? Why is my child slowly killing herself? Why is my child turning away from her family? Why is my child wayward from You?"

I love Job's comment in chapter 29:1–6,

> "Oh, how I long for the good old days, when
> God took such good care of me. . . . Oh, how
> I miss those golden years when God's friend-
> ship graced my home, When the Mighty One
> was still by my side, and my children were all
> around me, when everything was going my
> way, and nothing seemed too difficult." (MSG)

I miss those days. I get sad when I think back to how things were. How did things go so wrong? Get so off track? I too have a "face blotched red from weeping" and "dark shadows under my eyes" (Job 16:16 MSG). And yes, like Job said many times, I hate my life as a parent of an addict. I, like Job, wanted answers from God and was laying it all out on the table.

The part of Job's story that is often left out is that there is real spiritual warfare going on. In the book of Job, from the very beginning, God is in full control and is fully victorious, but the devil is fighting. He is fighting against God through every verse and still today. Sometimes my human life gets caught up in this spiritual warfare. For reasons I do not understand, the devil makes his strike. I feel like God is not to be found anywhere. But God has won the battle, and His angel armies are all around me fighting against things I do not comprehend.

While on earth I will never understand the battles being played out in the heavenly realms. But I do know that God uses those attacks and the human suffering I entail to carry out His successful plan. God's own Son suffered more than any human could, and His Son was perfect, utterly blameless. Jesus experienced immense pain, suffering, and separation from God, but Christ understood the spiritual battle before Him and the victory that was ahead of Him. Christ knew those same feelings I go through when I am suffering. He even asked for "the cup to be removed" (see Matt. 26:27). Yet Christ knew God's will, and Christ yielded to the Father's plan for His life because He knew the outcome of the battle.

Job couldn't see he was in the middle of a spiritual battle between the devil and God until God spoke to Job in a storm (see Job 38–41). Job realized God was always there. God was and is in complete control of the universe. God is victorious over the devil. God's plan will be completed. I think Job realized there was far more going on in the spiritual realms than he could understand. He recognized God's ways are beyond what the human mind can comprehend. Job did not see the whole picture in the midst of his suffering, but once God opened Job's eyes to His majestic ways, Job worshipped God and asked for forgiveness for not understanding.

Is it okay to question God about our suffering? Yes! Job did. David did. Many other followers of God did. But in the midst of pain, suffering, and uncomfortable circumstances, we must realize that God is greater than addiction. God is bigger than the suffering and pain. You must remember God is not picking on your family. Acknowledge there are battles in the heavenly realms being fought and won that you don't even know about. Life will not be easy—suffering will come—but draw as close to God as you can and know He has got this. You may ask why in the beginning, but conclude with "You have my family and me in the palm of Your loving hand."

> *Dear Lord,*
> *Thank You that You are a God I can ask and talk to about anything. Thank You that I can ask questions and make my requests known to You. Thank You that You know my thoughts before I even get them out of my mouth. Please help me, God, in this suffering and pain that I feel as I*

watch my child ruin her life with drugs. Thank You for fighting battles for me I don't even know about, Lord. Thank You that You know how this will end and it is all a part of Your plan. Thank You that I have a place called heaven where I will suffer no more. Thank You for always being present no matter how alone pain and suffering make me feel. It is just a mere feeling and not the truth. Thank You that whatever I am going through as a parent of an addict You will one day turn it all around, and Your great plan will be revealed.

Amen.

Questions for Thought

~ Why do I think this world should be perfect and my life should be easy?

~ Do I ever treat this world as permanent even though it is temporary?

~ Do I remember God is always present even when my pain and suffering are so big I can't feel God's presence?

~ Do I acknowledge that God's ways are not my ways, His thoughts not my thoughts?

~ Do I believe God is good and there are things in the spiritual realm I cannot understand, but God sees the whole picture and is working for the good of those who love Him?

~ Do I reach out to others suffering in similar situations and bring them peace and joy?

~ Do I worship God in the midst of my pain and suffering, knowing that my problems will "grow strangely dim" in the light of who God is?

Apathetic and Empty

> *"A thief comes only to steal and kill and destroy. I have come so that they may have life and have it in abundance."*
>
> JOHN 10:10

If you have a wayward child like me, you may have reached the point of apathy, the sense of pure emptiness. No matter what you do, you are butting your head against the wall, so why keep pushing? With an addict you are constantly fighting a rebellion. You ignore the feelings of rejection and hurt you first felt when your child went against your ways and instead grow numb. You stop caring just to avoid the pain. The "whatever" mode of thinking sets in. It is numbness full of selfishness and is worldly, showing a pure lack of faith.

During this apathetic time in my life, I wanted to blame my child for making me feel empty. After all, I would never have felt this way if she had not kept rebelling. Wrong! This emptiness and apathy are straight from the devil himself, who came to steal, kill, and destroy my faith and my joy. And I am responsible for leaving the door open for this notorious thief. I let my feelings of depression, sadness, anger, and resentment fill me to the brim. In fact, I let myself believe the devil's lie and let that snake steal my focus away from the source of my innermost being, Jesus Christ!

Yes, I was not happy with the way my child was choosing to behave, and I had a right to be angry. I had a reason to be frustrated. But I did not have the right to become apathetic! I did not have the right to become lukewarm about the situation. What I should have done was look up. My focus should have been on my Lord, who is big enough for my problems. He never left and never quit working. Yes, I was living in chaos and misery in my household, but my God was right there holding my hand. It was going to be in His timing that things worked out, not just for me but for the one who needed Him the most, my daughter. Instead I let the devil fill me with doubt and emptiness every time things went wrong. I believed the devil's lie that things would never change and that I might as well give up.

God does not want our lives to be void, full of apathy and emptiness. We need to get on our knees and pray! Admit whatever you are feeling to God because He understands. He wants to listen, no matter what you are thinking and feeling. He wants you to trust Him and to lay your feelings and concerns at the cross. Now, things may not get better, things may not change, and they may even get worse, but do not become numb in your faith! Look up! Draw a line in the sand, and quit listening and believing Satan's lies. The times you don't think God is there, keep breathing and remember where that breath comes from. Remember His grace is sufficient! Above all else, pray without ceasing and cast all your worries on Him. You may have to be still sometimes, but you don't have to be empty. God would rather you be frustrated yet focused on Him. You may be scared and tired of the battle, but focus on your Commanding Officer and following through to the bitter end, win or lose! Do not allow the devil to steal, kill, and destroy, for Christ came that you may have life and live it to the full!

> *Dear Lord,*
> *Thank You for working through the problems in my family. Thank You for allowing me time to see Your glorious work! Forgive my apathetic feelings and doubt, thinking that things would ever change. Thank You for not "spewing me out of your mouth" like I deserved! Thank You for feelings, no matter how painful they are sometimes. Guard me against feeling desperate! Let that feeling sound an alarm that You are a faithful Redeemer of all! Do not let me be controlled by my feelings. Help me choose to ignore the devil's lies. Help me choose the life You came to give. I thank You that I can experience a full life in the midst of a dehilitating storm because I am anchored by You.*
> *Amen.*

Additional Scripture References

> Let us not get tired of doing good, for we will
> reap at the proper time if we don't give up.
> (Galatians 6:9)

Questions for Thought

~ Have I allowed the chaos from having a drug-
  addicted child to settle me into a state of apathy
  and emptiness?

~ Have I given up on my child, or even worse, have
  I given up on God?

~ Who is the real culprit is in this horrible situation,
  and why do I allow myself to sit at the devil's table
  instead of dining with Jesus?

~ Have I asked God to clear my eyes, open my ears,
  and cleanse my calloused heart so I may live fully
  even in the midst of a crisis?

Where Are You, God?

My God, my God, why have you abandoned me?
Why are you so far from my deliverance
and from my words of groaning?
My God, I cry by day, but you do not answer,
by night, yet I have no rest.

PSALM 22:1–2

H ave you ever been in need of an answer to a problem or needed help with an issue, and God seemed to be out to lunch? That is a rather rough question for a Christian to be asking, isn't it? If each of us was honest, we have all felt that way at one time.

Sometimes I feel like God has left the building, but I am the one who has changed in our relationship. I have gone my way and left God out of the equation. It only seems like He is not there, when in fact, He has and continues to be there all along. I am guilty of walking away from God, but He has never abandoned me. At other times it seems everything I am doing is in line with God. I am praying, studying His Word, trying to do the best I can, yet the answer does not come; the solution will not reveal itself.

During the years my family has been plagued with a child battling drug addiction, I have often felt God was far away. It has been well over four years since the drug addiction nightmare began with my child. Sometimes our prayers were answered immediately, but other times prayers just seemed to go unheard or ignored by God. I sometimes thought God was just letting us figure it out on our own. Over the last few years, I have questioned God and the plan He had for my life. My circumstances did not seem to fit the "Christian plan." We were supposed to have the American Dream, not a complete nightmare. I guess somewhere in my tiny brain I thought everything would be smooth sailing in life, and "those types of things" only happen to those who needed to get back on track or to those who did not follow God.

No way would I ever say we were the perfect Christian family! We all fall short and seek our own way. But compared to the world's standards, we assumed we had it right. So when we first began to have trouble with our daughter and her drug issues, we prayed. We prayed for her to turn away from this sin and prayed God would change her life. We prayed for a rededication of her life to God since she was already a Christian. At times prayers seemed to be answered, and we thought she coming back. She even thought she was getting right with

God, but eventually she would fall off the wagon and return to letting the monster of drugs rule her life. We prayed more. We prayed again and again. We had our whole extended family and closest friends praying. Even strangers were praying. But we did not see a total deliverance, and things seemed to get worse—family fights, police calls to the house, minor arrests for under-age drinking, drug use, etc. Out of complete desperation I screamed at God, "*Why* is this happening? Where are You? Do You hear me? Answer this prayer now!" That sounds like a modern-day psalm from David, doesn't it?

I felt like I was doing everything God wanted me to do in the situation. I knew well He could heal her disease in an instant (or at least quickly), but the healing just had not come. Thinking and asking God these questions made me feel crummy about myself as a Christian. I should not have been asking God this! I knew He was there, and I knew He loved me. He died on the cross for me. What more could I ask, right?

These thoughts and feelings have gnawed at my gut for years now. Not that along the way God has not shown Himself to me or let me know He was there. He has done that time after time, through friends He has provided for me, through messages in Scripture, through sermons on Sunday mornings, even through strangers on the street. It might be a kind word. It might be a special verse someone sends. It might be a stranger or friend telling me their story about how addiction affected them and how God came through for them. I have had God moments, yet my problem has not been fixed. I have often thought, *When am I going to get my miracle—my answered prayer?* I have even thought, *Well this is God's will for my life.*

I might as well just accept it. But that thought goes against everything I know and believe about God. I don't believe God wants my daughter to be an addict or our family to suffer the way we have.

Then one day I realized my problem. My desire to have this pain taken away immediately had impeded me from believing God would answer my prayer one day. Because He was not working in my timing, I was choosing to believe He was not there. He had never been "out to lunch" during my prayers about my daughter's addiction. He has been, is, and will continue to be right there with me for as long as it takes for His greatest glory to be revealed.

A sermon from an associate pastor at my church confirmed to me I needed to have faith in God's plan and continue praying. I had to believe my daughter would be delivered from addiction to the saving grace of God. I had to thank God for the miracles He was already performing in my life and in her life. I had to continue to be faithful in what I could not yet see.

I believe in a God I cannot see. I believe in a heaven I cannot see. And if I can believe in those, I can believe His plan for my daughter and for me is all for the best. I can believe He will finish what He started. I can believe He is right here with me, carrying me to a place of healing, peace, and love.

Reflect on who God is and what He had done for you. You know God is great. You know He has helped you with things in the past. You have seen Him work miracles in your family's life and in the life of your friends. You are a child of God. Continue to breathe in and out. Continue to study His Word. Continue to pray. Remember God will answer your prayers in

His timing. Believe God will conquer all evil, and know ultimate healing will occur in heaven, if not on this earth.

> *Dear Lord,*
> *Thank You for being there! Thank You for*
> *allowing me to ask why? Thank You that You*
> *have provided examples of people in the Bible You*
> *dearly love that asked You the same questions I*
> *do now. Thank You for showing David's openness*
> *with You in Your Word and for sending Your*
> *Son to give us an even better picture of how to*
> *be in relationship with You. Both in examples*
> *of humanness, pain, and grief felt forsaken, yet*
> *they were not! You completed in them what You*
> *started. Thank You for the miracle of healing You*
> *are doing in my life and in my child's life. For*
> *Yours is the power and glory forever.*
> *Amen.*

Additional Scripture References

GOD, how long do I have to cry out for help before you listen? How many times do I have to yell, "Help! Murder! Police!" before you come to the rescue? (Habakkuk 1:2 MSG)

Questions for Thought

~ Is it okay for me to question God? It is it okay for me to cry out to Him in anguish and despair?

~ Do I truly believe God is hearing my prayers and working on the answers in His timing? Or do I believe the God that sent His one and only Son to die on the cross for me no longer cares? Does it make sense that He would let His Son die on my behalf and then ignore me?

~ Am I trying to make God work on my time line when He is the Author and Controller of time?

~ Can I trust the waiting and silence are all in God's hands and deliverance will come at the perfect time?

Lack of Faith

> *Jesus said to him, "'If you can'? Everything is possible*
> *for the one who believes." Immediately the father of*
> *the boy cried out, "I do believe; help my unbelief!"*
>
> MARK 9:23–24

As a parent of a child who struggles with drug addiction, I have watched my child wither away physically. I noticed the change in her cognitive processes and experienced her emotional and behavioral changes. Even worse, I suffered the loss of the relationship I had with her. Watching the physical, mental, emotional, and spiritual illness addiction has created in my child is gut-wrenching. It is as if she has been possessed by something that cannot be expelled. I am watching my child commit slow suicide, and I can do nothing to stop it.

I have prayed and prayed for God to heal my daughter of addiction. I have had numerous prayer warriors pray for her. I have sent her to rehabs, doctors, and counselors. I have experienced the pain of giving "tough love," hoping she would come to her senses.

After I did all I knew to do and the answer to my prayers seemed distant and unlikely to happen, I doubted if God was listening. I heard stories of miraculous healing from drug addiction. If God did that for one person, maybe He would do it for my daughter. But that was not and is not the way God is working in her life. This process has been a test of my faith, and to be honest, I have been found lacking.

Deep down I know God has to be listening and has to be working behind the scenes in ways I cannot see or understand. But I have days where everything seems to be coming apart at the seams. I have days when I think nothing will ever get better. Sometimes I don't think I can continue, and I tell God, "If You would heal her, everything would be okay!"

In my exasperation God showed me a verse that hit home: Mark 9:24. In this chapter a father asks Jesus to heal his son from a demon that has possessed him since he was a young child. The father says to Jesus, "If you can do anything do it, have compassion on us and help us" (v. 22). Jesus replies to the father that believers have no "ifs" because God can do anything. The father exclaims he believes and asks Jesus to help him with his unbelief.

So, like this father in Mark, I believe God will heal my daughter one day in His way and in His timing. I will ask God to help me with my doubts. If you continue to read Mark 9 through verse 29, you discover the importance of prayer in the healing process, and so I will not quit praying. As a former addict taught my husband, I will continue to PUSH (Pray Until Something Happens.) As I am going through this trial, I will remember that God is with me and is always faithful.

> *Dear Lord,*
> *Please forgive my disbelief. Take away my*
> *doubt, especially when all hell breaks loose and the*
> *battles against addiction seem to be lost. Thank*
> *You for answering my call. Give me peace and*
> *reassurance while I am waiting.*
> *Amen.*

Questions for Thought

~ Do I question Jesus's ability to heal my child of addiction and rescue my family from the effects of addiction?

~ Do I stand firm in my belief that my almighty God can do anything?

~ Have I obeyed the Lord's command to trust Him and believe in not just His name but in what He can do while continuing to ask the Lord to help me with my unbelief?

~ Can I say in faith it is done and continue to pray until the mountains move?

Hopelessness

> *Be brave. Be strong. Don't give up.*
> *Expect GOD to get here soon.*
> PSALM 31:24 MSG

Hope will make you feel excited and expectant of what will come. It will replace anxious thoughts and fears with optimism. Having hope is easy when things are going well. Then in the darkness there is hopelessness. It will make you feel defeated and like there is no use in trying because it is already over. It is death to the heart and soul.

While writing this, I am forty-seven years old, and my daughter is twenty. I have been writing these devotions since I was forty-four, and we are still battling with addiction and rebellion in my family. Let me tell you, I know how hopelessness feels. Sometimes my only hope was that nothing worse would happen. I have reached the pit of hopelessness and wallowed in it. It stinks! It is hell on earth.

But I know feeling hopeless is wrong. Job, David, and many others in the Bible had tastes of hopelessness, but they never stayed in the pit. They always remembered who and what their hope was in: God. Christ died on the cross and on the third day rose again to save us and give us hope. From the time of Christ's death until He was resurrected, everything seemed hopeless. The Bible says He descended into hell. That is utter despair. But God's power is greater than despair because Christ was resurrected. Praise God!

Romans 15:13 says, "May the God of green hope fill you up with joy, fill you up with peace, so that your believing lives, filled with the life-giving energy of the Holy Spirit, will brim over with hope!" (MSG). God knows our bodies and souls will experience seasons of hopelessness. Yet, if we are saved, the Holy Spirit, the same power that rose Jesus from the grave, lives in us. The Holy Spirit can fill us with hope again. We must not forget that. We must remember hope when it seems like nothing will ever change. We must be brave, with God's mighty shoulders to support us and His gentle hands to guide us. We must stand on God's promises. We must expect God to get here soon. We must live in hope rather than hopelessness. We must pray Romans 15:13, that God will fill us with joy and peace, fill us with the life-giving energy of the Holy Spirit so our lives will brim over with hope.

Dear Lord,

Thank You for sending Your Son to die on the cross to give me and all who call upon Him hope. Forgive me for listening to the devil's lies that there is no hope for my child. Help me be brave and stand on Your Word. Help me expect You to show up in Your great timing. I thank You that You are bigger than this addiction. Thank You for my child and the blessing she has been to me, even in the bad times. I thank You that Your love for my child is greater than my own. I thank You that You will remember my child and answer my prayer because Your Word says You will. I may be like Abraham and never see my hope fulfilled, but when I get to heaven, I will experience the fullness of hope and see Your plan accomplished. I know You have a plan for my life and my child's life. I know You did not strike us with addiction. As he did with Job, the devil is trying to pull my child and me away from You. I, like Job, will crawl out of my sense of hopelessness and will declare You as my hope.

Amen.

Questions for Thought

~ Have I given up hope? Am I surrendering to hopelessness? Am I in a pit of depression?

~ Do I believe in the power of the cross? Do I believe in the power of Jesus?

~ Do I seek Christ as the source of all hope, and is my hope not in this present world but resting in my future home in heaven? Do I believe, no matter what happens, God has a hope and future for my child and me in heaven?

~ Can others can see Christ in me by the overflowing hope I have in my life?

~ Is my hope greater than addiction, or am I going to let addiction win?

Listening

> *"Let anyone who has ears listen."*
> MATTHEW 13:9

I am not a good listener . . . at all. I get easily distracted by things going on around me. What I see and how I feel often deafen my ears to what I should be hearing. I may hear you, but I usually have to concentrate really hard to genuinely listen. I find it especially hard to listen to God when I am not seeking Him fully because His voice is not always audible.

Over the last several years I have been distracted by what I see my daughter doing and have been overwhelmed by the emotions and feelings over having a wayward child. I find it hard to listen to normal conversations at work and even to friends and family because I am so in tune to the negative noise in my life. I often have realized that I hear a person talking to me but have no clue what that person is saying because I was not listening.

When you have a wayward child, not only are everyday conversations difficult to focus on, but listening to God can feel impossible. I found myself talking and praying to God, reading the words God spoke through the Scriptures, but not listening to what was being said.

When I first began to suspect that my daughter was using drugs, I prayed for God to let it not be true. I frantically looked for evidence in her room when she was not around. I questioned her and her friends. I can even remember my husband and me following her at night in our car. I thought I was vigilant in my pursuit to find answers, and when I could not find reason for her rebellious behavior, I could only ask God to tell me what I needed to know. I needed God to hear me, and I needed to listen for His answer. Believe it or not, I believe I did audibly hear God one night. I was asleep and suddenly awoke. I sat up straight in bed as if someone had called my name. Then I heard God tell me, "Your daughter is doing drugs." I not only heard it, but you can be sure I listened. Not long after that we found out from our daughter that she had been drug tested at school and was more than likely going to fail. I was listening for sure at that point.

All of that was at the initial stages of our journey with addiction. Things just got worse from there. Numerous battles with our daughter, fights in our marriage, turmoil with our other child, and confusion and chaos all around distracted our listening. During those times it was hard to hear what God was telling us to do. Even today, when I get caught up in my feelings, I cannot hear God. I guess I have my "worry" fingers stuck in my ears so I do not have to listen.

God talks to me through His Word, through other Christian, through music, through dreams, and within my heart and soul. He is not always audible, but I must clear my heart and mind of all that is not from God—worry, fear, anxiety, lies, deceit, anger, and denial—in order to hear Him. If I am a Christian, Christ lives in me. I should be able to hear someone who lives in me, right? Matthew 13:16 states that we have special ears blessed by God to hear. That means I have the Holy Spirit in me now and a direct link to hear/listen to what God is saying. I can't hear Him with of all the clutter and noise from emotions and feelings, and I can't hear Him when I have fingers stuck in my ears because I'm afraid it might be hard to deal with what God has to say.

You must totally clear your cluttered heart and mind to hear what the Holy Spirit is telling you. You must be still and patient to listen to God. He often whispers and waits for you to quiet down to listen to Him. I am still working on my listening, but it is becoming easier as I learn to recognize the background noise. I can then start to turn that ugly noise down and tune into God. I am hopeful that one day my ears will be completely transformed into "God-blessed ears." I can only imagine how listening through those kind of ears will change my relationship with Christ and my relationship with others for the better.

Dear Lord,

Forgive me for being so distracted with the sounds of this world and the words from the devil. Forgive me for not listening to You first and foremost. Help me settle quickly when those calls from my wayward child come so that I may listen and hear what You would have me do as a parent.

Amen.

Additional Scripture References

"For this people's heart has grown callous; their ears are hard of hearing, and they have shut their eyes; otherwise they might see with their eyes, and hear with their ears, and understand with their hearts, and turn back— and I would heal them. Blessed are your eyes because they do see, and your ears because they do hear." (Matthew 13:15–16)

Questions for Thought

~ Do I find it hard to hear from God?

~ Am I only listening to the clutter of the world and to my own feelings and emotions?

~ Have I asked God to open my "God-blessed ears" to hear Him and Him only?

~ Have I settled, gotten still, and focused on what God is telling me, teaching me, reminding me, and revealing to me through His Word, through other believers, and through His still, quiet voice?

~ Am I listening, ready to respond, knowing that He knows best, or do I have my fingers stuck in my ears because of my self-absorption?

Disappointment

> *Though the fig tree does not bud and there is no fruit*
> *on the vines, though the olive crop fails and the fields*
> *produce no food, though the flocks disappear from the pen*
> *and there are no herds in the stalls, yet I will celebrate in*
> *the LORD; I will rejoice in the God of my salvation! The*
> *LORD my Lord is my strength; he makes my feet like those*
> *of a deer and enables me to walk on mountain heights!*
>
> HABAKKUK 3:17–19

Overcoming the deep disappointment of your own flesh and blood rebelling against everything you have taught them feels impossible. It is so hard to find joy or sing praises all while trying to process what feels like the loss of your child. A child's suffering will break your heart.

I remember when my scary suspicion was confirmed My daughter was showing all the classic symptoms of using drugs. She was confining herself to her room, losing interest in activities she used to find fun, sleeping a lot, showed declining grades, changing friendships, and having an overall rotten attitude. God woke me up in the middle of the night, and He told me that my daughter was doing drugs, and two days later she came to us and revealed she had been drug tested at school and was more than likely going to fail. My heart dropped. Our world was about to change forever.

My daughter was an honor-roll student throughout middle school. She cheered in middle school and her freshman and sophomore years in high school, as well as on a competitive team, and dreamed of being a cheerleader in college. I never pressured her about her grades or whether she cheered. These were things she wanted and worked hard at achieving.

Her group of friends changed during her freshman year of high school. Her grades dropped with each nine weeks from freshman year through sophomore year. Cheerleading became less important, and she would always try to find an excuse to miss competitive cheer practice. With the confirmed drug issue, she stopped cheering at the end of her sophomore year and struggled for the rest of high school to even make it into a college because of her grades. But these were minor, insignificant issues compared to our family conquering this now dooming drug problem. Disappointment is almost an understatement. I was devastated! Everything I had done to nurture and develop in my daughter was now ravished by drugs. My so-called perfect family life seemed destroyed. Our plans for the future and our finances stunted.

Thank goodness God understands. I found comfort in Habakkuk 3:17–19. Even though the verses are talking about crops and farm animals, these represent things of value. They are examples of things you spend time nurturing, tending to, loving, and anxiously waiting to bloom, mature, and grow. I could see the parallel; my daughter would not blossom or grow the way I had dreamed or the way I had planned. It was evident my plans and goals were not a part of God's plan. I do not think my daughter's choosing to do drugs was God's plan, but it was her choice/decision, and God now had to help us through it. And that is why the second part of the verse is so beautiful! My daughter will speak of wanting to change and will temporarily make small changes. When this happens, I know deep down she does not want to be an addict, and I try to focus on these glimpses of hope that one day she will realize her lifestyle must change. Because of God's Word, I can count on Him to prevail, and I have this hope as my strength.

I am thankful now and then when I see her realizing her life is not what it is meant to be. I keep hoping she will lay her guilt, shame, and addiction down at the foot of the cross. He will win this fight we are struggling with. I am counting on God to restore my daughter and my family. That is the reason I can be joyful and sing praise. I am protected like the deer because I have a place to run when things get rotten and empty, and I am like the king of the mountain because my God is ultimately victorious over the world.

Dear Lord,

I hate being disappointed, especially about my child. I can only imagine how You feel when we disappoint You. Please forgive me for all the times I don't measure up, all the times I fail to bloom and when I produce rotten fruit, all the times I let the sheep pens and barns stay empty. I thank You that You rule and I don't. I thank You for being my Provider, my Hope, my Strength. I thank You that You will be victorious in the life of my child who is a Christian, one of Your children. I love You, Lord.

Amen.

Questions for Thought

~ Even though my life is not going as planned and things are not as they should be, am I praising God anyway?

~ Am I counting on God's rule to prevail?

~ Can I cling to that promise and gain strength, be free, and know I am more than a conqueror through Christ? Or am I going to wallow in the loss of the things of this world?

DAY 23

Speak Life

> *"I call heaven and earth as witnesses against you today*
> *that I have set before you life and death, blessing and curse.*
> *Choose life so that you and your descendants may live."*
> DEUTERONOMY 30:19

One of the things I have come to regret while in the stormy midst of my child's drug addiction has been the words I have spoken to her. As a parent of a child with an addiction, you are at times overcome with fear, anger, fatigue, selfishness, and so forth. Your heart becomes polluted with these feelings and characteristics, so from out of nowhere, in the midst of a confrontation or a normal conversation, come these vile words that seem to vomit from your mouth onto your child. I have said some nasty things to my child out of the fruit in my heart, fruit not of the Holy Spirit but fruit I had planted and sown.

Luke 6:45 states, "A good person produces good out of the good stored up in his heart. An evil person produces evil out of the evil stored up in his heart, for his mouth speaks from the overflow of the heart." What we say will reveal our spiritual condition. Yes, even Christians can have a foul spiritual condition. Just because we are saved does not mean our heart is not blocked and our mind is not corrupted. When our hearts and thoughts are turned toward the world, what we say will not bear the fruit God wishes us to produce. It will lack His attributes of grace, mercy, love, and power. Instead, we will speak from the fear, anger, fatigue, selfishness, and hopelessness bottled up inside of us because our focus is turned to the storm of addiction.

Even more than the addiction, things in our own personal lives have created these heart blockages, these emotional walls, and these lies in our minds that spill forth when circumstances in life don't go our way. A good example is how angry we become in heavy, crazy traffic conditions. That person that violated our driving route does not deserve the thoughts, words, and/or gestures we may display toward them. Those actions result from a much deeper issue within us. In the same way, your child that speaks, thinks, and behaves horrifically because of the intoxication of the drugs, truly does not deserve to be yelled at and cursed upon. That child may need loving discipline but not evil words spoken over them.

The words we speak have power—power to promote life or power to cause death. Words are what started the downhill spiral of my daughter way back in kindergarten when she was ridiculed for being "so little." Those seemingly meaningless words landed in her soul, and she defined herself by those words, thus, bringing death to the abundant life God called her to. She built up walls emotionally and hardened her heart to prevent the pain, which eventually caused her to do anything to fit in—even trying drugs (something she vowed she would never do). Little did she know the path of destruction ahead of her. The words we spoke over her because of our own desperation to help her and our own sinful hearts did nothing but continue the death cycle of her soul and spirit. We did speak life-giving words over her as we were raising her—we were not monsters—but when drugs entered the picture, everything changed, and we often lost control of our tongues. Thankfully, through a small group at our church, my husband and I learned about the power of our words and how speaking life could change our home environment and our relationship with our daughter, even though our circumstance did not change. Our recognition of the power of our words became the difference. We realized we could bless the situation with God's presence, or we could curse it with our own worldly ways. To speak life means speaking over our daughter as God called her to be, speaking truth over the situation, and allowing God's power to intervene through our words. For instance, the emotion anger was still present but not the vile words. Discipline was present but out of love and not verbal abuse. By speaking life over our daughter and our situation, we were stopping the lies the enemy had planted in each of us. Using God's promises in His Word and speaking them over our circumstances allowed His power to change our feelings, heart, and thoughts even in a seemingly impossible situation.

My hope is that as you read this devotion, you will be able to be proactive from now on with your words over your child and your situation.

So how do you do it? You must surrender your heart to Christ by totally cleaning your heart of all the judgments and sin you have allowed to take root. You must surrender to the words of God and speak as Jesus did with truth and grace. Jesus did this with the woman at the well. Truth and grace yield conviction, not condemnation. Conviction brings forth repentance because of the kindness of God not to condemn us. Conviction shows us our problem but provides a way out. It is life-giving. It allows healing and deliverance. It is restoring. God can free us to live a full, abundant life.

Second, you must be slow to speak, slow to anger, and quick to listen as stated in James 1:19. By doing these three things, we are able to gauge our tongues, control our thoughts, and keep our hearts pure. Accordingly, if you have a child with a drug addiction, you should just automatically know that some pretty irrational thoughts and evil language are going to come out as a result of the drugs. But remember this is not the person; it is the drugs! So curse the drugs and the true enemy (Satan), not your child. Sometimes difficult things must be confronted and addressed.

Furthermore, you must not let your feelings get in the way of your words. You must be obedient to God and strive to control your tongue. Proverbs 18:21 states, "Death and life are in the power of the tongue, and those who love it will eat its fruit." Our tongues will fail us when we speak from the overflow of a "worldly" or "fleshy" heart. Our tongues will produce fruit when we speak from the abundant Holy Spirit-filled heart. When our hearts are aligned with the Holy Spirit, we will seek to be in God's Word, we will practice taking evil thoughts captive, and we will be able to control our tongues more effectively.

> *Dear Lord,*
>
> *I confess, Lord, that I have spoken evil, vile things from my mouth and directed them toward my child and family. What I have spoken is simply not true, and it only agrees with what Satan would want me to believe. My words have not indicated what You, Lord, say about me or my child. Lord, I repent of speaking from judgment and condemnation. I turn away from that and seek life-giving words and conviction toward my child, my family, and myself. I release these wicked words to You. In the name of Jesus, I command Satan to leave my thoughts, feelings, and flee from my mouth. I submit my words to align with You, Lord. Lord, thank You for forgiving me and cleansing my tongue. Just as You have called heaven and earth and You have set before me life and death, blessing and cursing, I choose life so that I and my descendants may live life abundantly (paraphrase of Deut. 30:19).*
>
> *Amen.*

Questions for Thought

~ Am I speaking life over my child and my situation, or am I speaking a death sentence?

~ Am I finding it difficult to guard my thoughts and control my tongue?

~ What can I do to take captive my thoughts and gauge my tongue?

~ Is anything within me keeping me from God's Word and from aligning myself to His promises?

~ Am I spending time in God's Word and allowing it to renew me?

PART III

Anchored

So you have thrown in your anchor, and you have gone deep with God. You have given Him your anger and your guilt. With an open heart you have received forgiveness and have forgiven. Courageously you have surrendered your fears and substituted His strength for your weakness. You have acknowledged spiritual warfare and are ready to battle as a mighty warrior of God. You have cast all your worry and anxiety unto Him. You have found rest. You expect pain and suffering to come in this world, yet you can stand firm and survive with God at your side. You have relinquished apathy and emptiness to the grave and strive to live a full life. You have renewed your faith and cast off hopelessness. You are listening to God and can openly praise His name in spite of disappointment.

You can now be anchored to the Rock in the midst of this storm of addiction with your child. You may be swayed by the wind, rain, and waves to come, but your hope is in God alone. By being anchored by Him, you will have joy and thankfulness. You will run your race, you will know you are a part of God's plan, and you will know how deep and how wide God's love is for you.

DAY 24

Who Is My God?

"Our Father in heaven, your name be honored as holy."
MATTHEW 6:9

One of the defining moments as a parent of a drug addict that seasoned me during this trial was my discovery of who God really is and what a true relationship with Him looks like. I have been a Christian for many years, and I have had a fairly good relationship with God. He had always been someone I worshipped on Sundays. I had always prayed to God when I really needed something or was upset. If things had been going fairly well, my communication was daily but not constant. I was grateful for blessings bestowed and answers to prayers. Based on Scripture, I always knew God was there for me and would never leave me. Yet I had never experienced who God is, and my relationship with Him was more one-sided: my side mostly. To my surprise, once I realized the predicament the storm of addiction had placed me and my family in, I truly discovered God and the power source that He is. To know God intimately and to solely depend on Him has been my saving grace through this battle of addiction.

I would like to introduce you to the God I know and give you a glimpse of my deepened relationship with Him. First, do you know the names of God? The following are some of the Old Testament names of God and their meanings (adapted from Bible.org: *Names of God* by J. Hampton Keathley III):

El Shaddai: Lord God Almighty (Genesis 17:3)

El Roi: God of Seeing (Genesis 16:13)

Jehovah Nissi: The Lord My Banner (Exodus 17:15)

Jehovah Raah: The Lord My Shepherd (Psalm 23:1)

Jehovah Rapha: The Lord My Healer (Exodus 15:26)

Jehovah Shammah: The Lord Is There (Ezekiel 48:35)

Jehovah Shalom: The Lord of Peace (Judges 6:24)

Jehovah Jireh: The Lord Will Provide (Genesis 22:14)

Jehovah Mekoddishkem: The Lord Who Sanctifies You (Ezekiel 37:28)

One of the easiest ways to get close to God is by simply praising His name. Jesus in Matthew 6:9 teaches the disciples to begin prayer by recognizing and calling out to our Father in heaven. In doing so, we are automatically seeking the totality of God and His kingdom instead of seeking ourselves and our own agendas. By calling out to "Our Father," we are acknowledging His rightful place in our lives. We are proclaiming His holiness and His authority. God loves when we align ourselves to Him. An automatic intimacy forms because our hearts are now connected and communication can flow freely.

When you are in the midst of battling drug addiction with your child, it is easy to forget who God really is. Many parents in normal situations often worship their child more than they do God. As a parent of a child with a drug addiction, I definitely became obsessed with my child and my situation. I let it become bigger than my God. I created my own warped idol. And though God never left my side, I distanced myself far from Him. God never lost His grip on me, but He allowed time and experiences through the trials of drug addiction to teach me who He was and to increase the intimacy between us.

My hope is that as you read this devotion, you can be spared some of the hardships that come when we lose the knowledge of who God really is. I hope you will research the verses above for yourself and claim these names of God for yourself. Call upon the Lord by His many names. With these names come His promises and ultimately the intimate relationship you were always meant to have with Him no matter your circumstance.

Dear Lord,

Jehovah Nissi, the Lord my Banner, my rallying place and point of victory! You will be my place of victory in this drug war! Thank You for who You are—the great I Am! There is no other like You, God. Forgive me for allowing my child and her addiction to become bigger than You. Forgive me for not recognizing the power You bestow just in Your name alone. Thank You for Your gentleness in revealing who You are and not forsaking me as I deserve! Jehovah Shammah—The Lord Is There, always and forever.

Amen.

Questions for Thought

~ Who is my God?

~ Who and what am I worshipping/focusing on the most in this situation? Is it my child? The addiction? My circumstance?

~ Do I recognize the power in God's names and the promises of who He is in me and my situation as I call out His names in my prayer time with Him?

Joy

> *"Until now you have not asked anything in my name. Ask*
> *and you will receive, and your joy will be complete."*
> JOHN 16:24 NIV

I write this chapter at a time when I don't feel joy in human terms. Speaking from the flesh, I could not be in an unhappier place. My life is not at all what I dreamed it would be. My family is in complete upheaval, and if left up to my flesh, I would get out now. But these thoughts are all based on feelings of unhappiness and disappointment. This is definitely not the fruit of the Spirit.

Jesus says He came that all may have joy. I am a believer, and I must choose joy in the midst of my trials. I may not feel happy at present, but I have joy because Christ lives in me and He is the source of my joy even when I feel unhappy. As

Christians, we are never promised a life free of problems, sorrow, pain, or regret. Instead the Bible says we should be joyful during these times.

I have prayed and prayed in Jesus's name for my rebellious child to turn away from her sin. I have prayed that God would immediately heal my family. But those prayers have not been answered yet. The pain and trouble are still present.

God spoke to me through a song on the radio about someone going through a storm in life. In the main chorus of this song, the words expressed are basically that the person is going through a painful circumstance, and she doesn't know what on earth God is doing, but the singer exclaims that she still knows who God is.

This is joy in the midst of heartache. I must remember God is who He is today and forever. God is good. God is love. God is Healer. God understands. God answers my prayers. God's ways are not my ways. God's timing is His own and not mine. God knows the bigger picture. God saves. God is for me. For all of these reasons, I must choose to be joyful even in bad situations. I must make my requests in Jesus's name and know that my prayers have been heard and rejoice in that alone. I must remember that God is victorious over evil and that even if not on earth my peace and ultimate happiness and joy are waiting for me in heaven.

My wayward child can make me feel so unhappy. My child, however, is not my source of joy. My joy is from God. When my drug-addicted child leaves me feeling sad, I have to turn my focus to God and ask Him to fill me with joy. Then immediately thank God for all He has done in the past and for all He will do in the future for me, my child, and my family. I choose to thank Him for the little things that evoke feelings of happiness in my day such as a laughing baby, a funny joke, a timely call from a dear friend, the love of others in my family. I choose to reach out and serve others. Nothing brings greater joy than serving others and making others happy. I must keep my focus on God, not on my problems with my child. I give these problems to God. I pray every second if I have to, in order to keep the devil from stealing my joy.

> *Dear Lord,*
> *I feel so unhappy. I hate that I let the choices my child has made make me feel unhappy and leave me joyless. Forgive me for losing focus from You. I thank You that I know who You are, even though I don't get or understand what You are doing. In the midst of my trial, I ask that You fill my heart with Your joy! Thank You for being my source of joy.*
> *Amen.*

Questions for Thought

~ Am I relying on my situation with my drug-addicted child to change for me to have joy?

~ Do I know the difference between happiness and joy? Do I know that happiness is a feeling and that joy is the fullness of God living in and working through me?

~ Do I understand that I have to choose joy? Do I understand that I have to move away/run from darkness and unhappiness or I will fall into its pit?

~ Do I seek joy by looking for Jesus/God in my everyday world?

Thankfulness

> *We must be careful not to stir up discontent;*
> *discontent destroyed them.*
> 1 CORINTHIANS 10:10 MSG

We are to be thankful regardless of the circumstances. God's Word declares it, and I know I am to be content in all situations. But it is not the easiest task, and God does not like grumbling. This has caused me to stumble many times over the past few years. In the midst of experiencing the difficulties of a wayward child and journeying through the devastation of a loved one overcome by drug addiction, God wants me to approach Him with a heart of thankfulness. I know I am supposed to be thankful, but it can be difficult. It is not always my initial response, but God is teaching me to be thankful in all things.

I have hated and still hate what my daughter and my family have experienced over the past several years. I have grumbled and complained to God in the midst of praying for relief and deliverance from this horrific situation. I guess you would say I was acting like one of those Israelites wandering in the desert. I was following God, but I hated the situation He seemed to have put me in. I was complaining about how horrible everything was, and I was pleading for Him to help me get out of this situation and to turn my daughter back to the way she was before.

Grumbling and complaining put me in a dark pit I desperately wanted out of. God showed me how grumbling and complaining only deepened my pain and depression. Through devotions, church sermons, and people, God reminded me of His sovereignty. He taught me to be thankful in all my circumstances. Thank goodness it was God showing me instead of someone else. Only God would have the patience and forgiveness to teach me this lesson because I kept going back to grumbling and complaining even when He was showing me the way through "this desert" I was traveling. Anyone else would have quit on me, given up on my unteachable spirit.

Initially, through the first episodes of dealing with a wayward child with drug addiction, I was in such pain and shock I was constantly crying at my own pity party. I could not muster up an ounce of thankfulness even though I had been reading my Bible and I knew I should be thankful in all situations. But God was merciful toward me. One day I heard His still small voice say to me, "Just be thankful you are breathing. Just breathe in and out today. Just be grateful I provide you air and a working body to breathe." And that was the first time I could thank God in the midst of pain and turmoil.

The next thing God showed me was life through His eyes. When you are looking at life through human eyes in the midst of trouble, things are gray, dull, and stagnant. God asked me to look for Him in the world around me. God is not gray, dull, or stagnant. So I looked for things He created in this world for me to enjoy: beautiful sunsets, the night sky full of stars, a beautiful flower, a cute puppy, a giggling baby, a deep soulful patient I was working with, chirping birds, and soft, sweet breezes. I was thankful for the little things God was providing for me during this terrible time—things only He could create. Things that showed me He was in control. Many of these things I could be thankful for when everything else was bleak. Through being thankful, I was able to creep out of the pit to find joy and laughter again—another thing I could be thankful for.

After a while, when I would grumble and fall back into the emotional pit, I would force myself to find something to be thankful for. It might be hearing of a situation worse than mine and being thankful my daughter was still alive. It might be thankfulness for the essentials like food, clothing, and a roof over my head. It might be thankfulness for the husband, son, and family I have. It might be thankfulness for the job I have where I can help others and be away from my life for a moment. It might be thankfulness for a kind stranger or for the wonderful friends God had given me in recent years. It has always been thankfulness for God's control in spite of our desperate situations. Before long, the pain and suffering were being dulled by my being thankful, and God's joy was replacing my human sorrow.

Not that I still don't have pity parties and I don't stumble into grumbling again. I do. But I now remove myself from those feelings before I fall into that terrible pit. Negativity is a black hole. Grumbling and complaining are a devil's trap of the soul. Being thankful cleanses a foul heart. It is praising God for who He is, was, and will be! It is a realization that God is in control. He is worthy of all my praise for He is good, and His love for me is everlasting, no matter what my situation is at the moment. Being thankful keeps me from self-destruction and protects me from the devil's evil.

God taught me to be thankful even when I did not think it was possible. Sometimes life is so cruel that I cannot find it in myself to be thankful. But God's greatness makes me thankful! I hope after reading this, you will ask God to show you how to be thankful. I know from experience He will. He hates grumbling and complaining. They do nothing for Him or for us. But being thankful brings honor and glory to God, and we cannot do that enough. He will show us how to be thankful if we seek His help.

> *Dear Lord,*
> *Thank You for teaching me to be thankful.*
> *Right now I thank You for not punishing me for*
> *my negative attitude and grumbling about the*
> *way I thought You were handling things. Father,*
> *thank You for returning my contentment in the*

midst of trouble. Most of all, thank You, Lord, for
a soft place to land when I fall.
    Amen.

Additional Scripture References

Hallelujah! Give thanks to the LORD, for he is good;
his faithful love endures forever. Who can declare
    the LORD's mighty acts
or proclaim all the praise due him? (Psalm 106:1–2)

Questions for Thought

~ Am I grumbling and complaining like the Israelites in the desert when God is right there showing me the way and providing for all my physical, emotional, and spiritual needs?

~ Am I thankful for Jesus's dying on the cross and saving me? Is there anything else He has to do?

~ What blessings has He poured down on me?

~ Am I so blinded by my child's addiction I cannot even see what God is doing and will do for me?

~ Have I asked God to show me how to be thankful in the midst of this circumstance?

DAY 27
Understanding

> *We don't yet see things clearly. We're squinting in a fog, peering through a mist. But it won't be long before the weather clears and the sun shines bright! We'll see it all then, see it all as clearly as God sees us, knowing him directly just as he knows us!*
>
> 1 CORINTHIANS 13:12 MSG

When we understand, we have a clear visual picture of what is happening, why it is happening, and the reason something is going on.

I have a hard time understanding why my daughter became a drug addict. In my mind I have concluded something must have happened to her in those teen years that caused a deep, painful wound. I don't know what it was. I only know from listening and reading between the lines of my daughter's communication with me that something happened and she cannot get over it. My guess is she uses drugs to avoid the pain and mental anguish over that life-crushing event. But it is only a guess. I do not have a real understanding of why she uses drugs.

As a Christian, I have had a difficult time understanding why drug addiction has struck our family. If you want me to be honest, I have trouble understanding how to deal with some of the issues that arise with loving a drug addict. It is hard to get a clear picture of what God is doing and what He wants me to do as a parent. It all gets cloudy and confusing at times, especially when you think your child has conquered the addiction, only to find out she relapsed into that ugly world again. So far we have been battling this addiction and rebellion in our family for more than four years, and I still don't get it!

I don't get how a beautiful blue-eyed, blonde girl, who was born with an adventurous personality bound by a heart of gold, could destroy herself as she does. I don't get how my child who has the world at her fingertips could just blow it all away for a drug rush. I do not understand how my "saved at six years old" daughter, my daughter who led others to Christ as a child, could be this far from God now. I do not understand why she keeps running from God when I know God is right there to rescue her if she would just surrender everything to Him.

In my mind I have guesses, intuition, and gut feelings about who, what, when, and why but no clear understanding of the whole picture. Frankly, I cannot see clearly enough through the fog of pain, disappointment, anger, and sadness at times to understand what God is doing. No, I haven't figured it out yet.

Thankfully, with God as my guide, I have found I'm not required to understand. For God's ways are not my ways. God is God, and I am me. With my strength I can only hold on to His Word and His promise there are reasons and a plan behind all this turmoil. In my power I can only trust all is being worked for good. I can only know God is here walking with me each day. I can only try to understand God's love and seek His wisdom. I can only hope one day I will understand all this chaos, and the chaos will be nothing but a beautiful picture my God created out of ashes.

> *Dear Lord,*
> *I cry out for the reason for all this. I do not understand, and I cannot get my head around it at times. Please just give me peace that surpasses all understanding each day. Let me experience You in the midst of my fog. Thank You that You understand even when I do not.*
> *Amen.*

Questions for Thought

~ Is it okay that I do not understand why my child is bound by drug addiction?

~ Will I trust God has the answers why, and He has the big picture, and it is complete?

~ Do I trust He will bring forth beauty from ashes?

~ Will I take the time to understand who I am in God and understand what God is to me in the midst of this turmoil?

Running the Race

> *Therefore, since we also have such a large cloud*
> *of witnesses surrounding us, let us lay aside every*
> *hindrance and the sin that so easily ensnares us. Let*
> *us run with endurance the race that lies before us.*
>
> HEBREWS 12:1

I wish I could tell you specifically how to finish this race we are in. The race a parent of a wayward child must run is long and treacherous. There are times of rest and refreshment along the way, but it is an uphill battle with a slippery downward slope, and bumps and bruises are plentiful.

Having a wayward child, a child bent on rebellion, a child whose body is ruled by drugs, a child whose soul is tricked by the demon of addiction, a child whose spirit is far from God, is a challenge. As a parent of this type child, you are running a race against things beyond your own physical and mental strength. But these things you are running against are not bigger than God. He is greater!

Some say God gives His toughest battles to His strongest warriors. Now, I'm not sure I am a fighter, and I do not feel strong. In fact, I feel like a worn, beaten-down slave at times. Yet, if I read of the saints before us like David and Daniel, I realize they were just plain people like me. God made them into warriors. They relied on God for strength and perseverance. These saints of old made huge mistakes and suffered in their lives even though they followed God. They became mighty warriors for God, and through them God fulfilled His plan. They finished the race before them by faith without ever receiving a prize here on earth.

As a Christian, I run the race with a piece of the prize, Christ, within me and ahead of me. My victory is because of the finished work of Christ, and I run my race through constant prayer for my child, endless unconditional love for my child, and constant cleansing of my heart and forgiveness of the offenses thrown my way. My race is run through living my life as an example of Christ for my child to see and through donning my spiritual weapons (truth, righteousness, peace, faith, and salvation) to finish the race against the devil.

So, yes, I am a parent of a wayward child. My child, I never quit praying for, was taken away from us because of drugs. I will not give up hope on her. I will run the race before me, for God is with me, and He wins the race for me. I will not let Satan get the best of my family or me during this trial. Even if the drugs take my daughter's life, I will continue to run the race. I will continue to run straight toward God and take as many with me as I can. I will run the race of helping as many parents with wayward children as I can. My race is to stay close to God in the midst of trouble, to be obedient to His ways, to love and help others as He has helped me. I cannot race to save my child from drugs—that is her race she must run. I can only stay my course, my race, and help others along the way. As a parent I can only love her, provide wisdom, and be an example of Christ to her.

Dear Lord,

Thank You for this race I love and hate at the same time. I hate the pain and discomfort from the race at times, but I love the closeness I have gained to You. I love the fact that I am victorious in You. I ask You to show me how to be a good parent to my wayward child. I ask You to give me wisdom on steps I need to take to draw her closer to You. I ask You to protect my child in her race. I ask You to get her attention so she may see You as the leader of her race and get off the path she is running toward. I love You, Lord.

Amen.

Questions for Thought

~ Am I in the race with Christ behind me, within me, and before me?

~ Do I know my part in this race even though I cannot control the other racers and the outcome?

~ Do I realize the race is already won, and all the saints in heaven are cheering me on to finish my part in the race? Do I hear those saints roaring in heaven for me not to quit no matter the difficulties and roadblocks?

God's Plan

> *"For I know the plans I have for you"—this is the*
> *LORD's declaration—"plans for your well-being, not*
> *for disaster, to give you a future and a hope."*
> JEREMIAH 29:11

This verse has been our family verse during these long, battling years with our daughter. We had this verse printed on her senior ad for her high school yearbook. My husband has this verse tattooed on his shoulder. We recall this verse in our times of struggle and doubt.

It has been several years since Ashlynn went to her first rehab at Teen Challenge in Arizona. She has been in multiple rehabs since, and she has seen several psychiatrists and medical doctors to help her with her addiction. It has been a never-ending journey. There have been brief glimpses of hope where we believed the battle was done and addiction of drugs had been replaced with an addiction to God. Once, she made it a month of being "clean," close to finding a job, looking for volunteer work, and going to church with us for four Sundays in a row. I thought, *This is it! She's got it*, only to be punched in the gut. She started doing drugs again. Same song and dance—being unusually sick, sleeping the days away, defiant attitude, nonchalant behavior, hanging with the old buds, and not leaving bad relationships when the opportunity arose.

My husband, son, and I were thoroughly frustrated and exhausted. Once again we had to enforce another horrible intervention, to demonstrate her choices would not change our principles or our lives. We had to tell her she could not be with us while under the influence of drugs. So time has passed with no communication and without seeing our daughter. It has been a time of grief, so difficult, so painful, yet strangely peaceful, knowing that God has this too. I love The Message Bible's version of Jeremiah 29:11: "I know what I'm doing. I have it all planned out—plans to take care of you, not abandon you, plans to give you the future you hope for." Sometimes how God works makes little sense in my mind. But the Holy Spirit reassures me He has this and will turn it all around.

There are verses in the Bible that declare this promise. Romans 8:28 states, "God works for the good of those who love him, who have been called according to his purpose" (NIV). Psalm 46:10 says, "Be still, and know I am God" (NIV). A new favorite verse I am claiming is Micah 7:7: "But me, I'm not giving up. I'm sticking around to see what GOD will do.

I'm waiting for God to make things right. I'm counting on God to listen to me" (MSG).

So I will continue to be obedient in my pain, and in my moments of doubt, I will seek His face. I will claim Jeremiah 29:11 and follow it with Micah 7:7.

> *Dear Lord,*
>
> *I know You have plans for me, not to harm me, and to give me the future I hope for. Amen. Amen. I am not giving up. I am sticking it through to the end to watch for Your beautiful redeeming plan to unfold. I know You hear my cry.*
>
> *Amen.*

Questions for Thought

~ Do I know God has a plan for my life and for my child's life?

~ Am I willing to follow God and take His lead for my life, or am I going to go my way?

God's Knowledge

> *You observe my travels and my rest;*
> *you are aware of all my ways.*
>
> PSALM 139:3

God knows everything about me. He knew me before I was in my mother's womb. He knows the number of hairs on my head. He knows my name. He knows my thoughts and my heart. He knows the universe and all of its makings because He is Creator of it all.

God knows the plan he has for me. He knows my good days and my bad days ahead. He is for me and not against me. He does not come to make my life miserable and heap trouble on me to see if I can muddle through it. He wants me to have a good future and to have hope.

Ultimately, as Christians, our future is in heaven, but I believe God wants me to have a future here on earth, even though it is temporary. We live in a fallen world, prowled by Satan. Satan does not want us to have hope or a future. Satan plans evil and wants to destroy us. So life here on earth will never be perfect. Our futures will not be perfect until we are in heaven. We will have trouble here on earth; God knows this and even tells us this in His Word.

God knows my daughter, and God knows me. He did not create my child to be an addict or me to suffer as a parent of an addict. My child made a bad choice for whatever reason. My child had something happen to her or within her that the devil used to pull her into his ways and pull her away from God's ways. God knows the plans He has for my daughter, and He is waiting for His prodigal daughter to come to her senses and return home.

God knows every terrible choice my daughter has made. He knows every terrible act I made. In this knowledge God still sent His Son, Jesus, to save me and my daughter. He offers me the gift of grace. He will not force it upon me; a gift is not forced onto anyone. You can only receive a gift if you accept.

God knows how this whole ordeal will turn out. He knows the next steps in His plan. It would be easy for God just to fix it immediately, and I know He has the power to do so, but He is waiting because He knows best. It is written He knows how to turn what was meant for evil into good for those who love Him (see Gen. 50:20). I will hold to God's knowledge being greater than what I know to sustain me through this crisis.

Dear Lord,

Thank You that You know everything! Thank You that You know my thoughts and my heart. Thank You for loving me anyway. Thank You for knowing the plans You have for me, and I know nothing will deter those ultimate plans. Thank You that the mistakes I make may lead me off the expected path temporarily, but You ultimately know the way if I follow. Thank You for loving my child and keeping her in Your sight and thoughts. Thank You that Your ways are greater. Thank You that You know how this is all going to end.

Amen.

Additional Scripture References

God, how precious your thoughts are to me; how vast their sum is! (Psalm 139:17)

Questions for Thought

~ Do I realize how much God loves me? Do I accept He knows me inside and out and still loves me?

~ Do I understand I live in a fallen world, and what happened to my child with drugs is not God's will? Do I know God is for me and not against me?

~ Can I accept and claim the gift of Jesus Christ as my Savior, my Redeemer? Can I rest in the fact that all those who believe in Him will be resurrected and forever be free of the chains this world places on us?

~ Can I agree God knows best, His plan is best, and I should follow Him all the days of my life no matter how this storm of addiction ends?

Afterword

I hope these devotions rescue you in the way they rescued me during this terrible trial in life. God blessed me in the midst of a crazy, mean storm. I found I could be calm, still, and anchored in His presence with a raging, stormy ocean of drug addiction surrounding me. At the time I began writing this devotional book, I hoped my daughter would come to her senses and be transformed and on fire for God, changing others' lives for the better. I have never stopped believing God would answer my prayer in His timing, but I had to get my focus on my Lord. I had some harsh lessons about trust, doubt, and God's sovereignty to learn as God held on to me and as I held on to Him in this storm. I had to become anchored by Him.

I need you to know God answered my prayer, but He answered it in the way He knew was best. My sweet Ashlynn was not healed here on Earth. Instead, she was healed on the other side of glory—in heaven—in the welcoming arms of her Lord and Savior, Jesus Christ. Ashlynn went to lead a drug-free life, healed in the presence of God on January 30, 2016.

I believe Ashlynn had great potential to live a life bringing others to the Lord. She was an amazing child who led many of her friends to Christ. She was a determined, strong-willed child that would have been a mighty warrior for God. The devil did not like this. She had some trials in her life growing up that wounded her deeply. The devil stepped in and began lying to her and confusing her thoughts. She experienced deep pain and sorrow and turned to drugs to numb her emotions—yet another scheme of the devil. The devil placed a stronghold on her that was overwhelming for a chemically altered brain. She had difficulty reasoning and rationalizing, making it challenging to overcome her addiction.

God showed up so many times during these five years to rescue her; she just could not hear Him or see Him because she was allowing the devil to speak louder to her than she was allowing God to speak. She understood God's capacity to forgive, and she could forgive others so easily, but she could not forgive herself, and this is where the devil kept her in chains. So many of us as Christians are trapped just like she was. We are free, but we choose to remain in the chains; we choose to believe the lies of the devil.

Ashlynn, I truly believe had an "addictive" brain. It took one time of doing drugs to fuel the fire. Once she took heroin, she was hooked, and her mind became so chemically altered she couldn't see any other way to survive life but to continue to use drugs. The devil thought he had won. He stole her joy and freedom she had in Christ, and he almost took my family and my freedom in Christ, but God showed me the battle was already won. He would heal her if not on earth then in heaven because she was a child of God. I think God knew He could best rescue her and save others through her death. God's ways are not our ways. His thoughts are higher than our thoughts. God is God, and I am not!

While her death is excruciating, I can indeed say it is not as painful as watching her live in the captivity of drugs. Drugs are a demon, and they reap hell on everyone. Seeing her in pain and trapped in hell on earth was awful. I think if Ashlynn could mentally submit all to God, she might have been healed here on earth. I know God knew there was no other way for her to be healed but in heaven. I believe through her death many lives will be changed and Jesus will be glorified. I believe if her life had been taken earlier, I would not be the person I am today. God took a terrible storm of drug addiction to anchor me so that when He brought her to heaven, I would be grounded and secure in this new trial of life here on earth— life with my daughter in heaven.

While I miss her terribly, and I get a "homesick" feeling when I think of her, I know where she is now; and I know she is free, happy, and at peace. She is smiling and full of joy. She is the person God always intended her to be now. That's what happens when we get to heaven: we are complete in Him, and we are finally home!

My prayer is for you to be anchored by God as you press on to the prize at the end of your storm. "We have this hope as an anchor for the soul" (Hebrews 6:19). I pray for protection and healing over you and your children. I pray for abundant peace as you submit yourselves and your child completely to the Lord. I pray for lives to be saved unto Him, for God ultimately wins, and God does heal!

About the Author

Deborah Bailey is the cofounder of the Ashlynn Bailey Foundation, and with her husband, Mike, they are committed to raising awareness and ministering to parents of addicts. Deborah and Mike reside in the Birmingham, Alabama, area with their son.

Davis

Davis

Davis